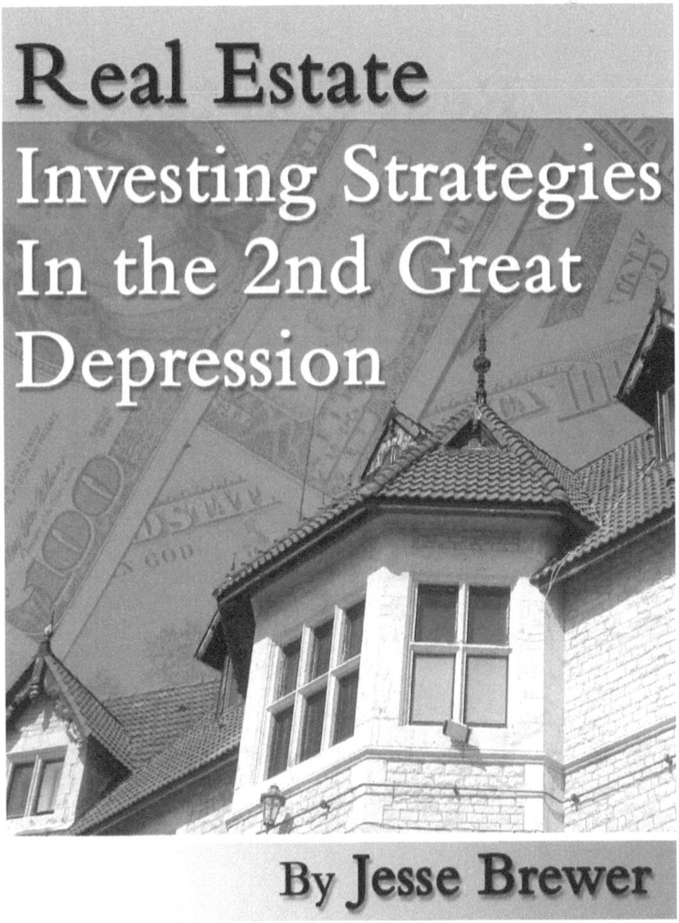

Real Estate
Investing Strategies
In the 2nd Great
Depression

By Jesse Brewer

Real Estate Investing Strategies In the 2nd Great Depression

By

Jesse Brewer

LEGAL NOTICE

EDITOR
ABC Writers, www.abcwriters.com

PUBLISHER
Createspace

Dedicated to every investor—past, present, and future—in America. Only by investing together in this country can we save our great nation.

Table of Contents

Introduction

I don't know what your real estate investment experience is, but I can tell you that I've never seen a more exciting time to buy and hold than in the past several years. With the current over-correction taking place with lending institutions, any would-be investor who doesn't know how to "think outside the box," and take advantage of these unusual conditions, is forced to sit on the sidelines. If you are able to get financing and get in the market and buy some of these great deals, now is the time and it has never been better.

Let me present it to you from a different angle. When people are buying equities, they buy stock when the price is on a downward trend (buy low) and then sell it on an upward trend (sell high). And what is real estate in general doing now? Across the country, in most instances, it is definitely in a *downward trend*. So why not buy it for 50-60 cents on the dollar and wait for the market to take an *upward trend* before you sell? People will always need a place to live, no matter what the state of the economy. Personally, I no longer invest in the stock market at all. I am into real estate primarily, with some of my investments in other arenas—but no money in stocks.

For reasons I outline below, the stock market will soon crash, and anyone investing money there is foolish. The baby boomers are starting to retire, and there are seventy-five million of them. Last year in this country, over seven hundred thousand people turned 59 ½. This means they are now able to cash in their 401K's without penalty. The stock market took six years to recover from the 9/11 terrorist attacks. A lot of people lost a lot of money in their pensions and 401k's during that period. They have also lost faith in the stock market and financial infrastructure in general. Once they are able to withdraw the money from their retirement accounts, many of them will do so.

Now consider the next generation, aka "Generation X", which is comprised of people born during the years 1965 to 1981 (approximately). The Gen-Xer's number only about fifty-one million, and they have far less money than the Baby Boomers. The Gen-Xer's are putting their money into stocks, 401k's and other financial infrastructure markets to save for their "retirement." But with seventy-five million Baby Boomers pulling money *out,* and fifty-one million Gen-Xer's putting money *in,* this amounts to a significant discrepancy: *far more money is coming out than going in.* And anyone who knows how a zero-sum market works can tell you this:

> *With such a huge disparity in the money flow, it will not be long before the stock market collapses.*

So how do these trends make real estate such a good investment? Consider the Millennials, which is the generation right behind the Gen-Xer's. With seventy-four million members, the Millennials are close to the Baby Boomers in size and volume of capital. Remember, with all three of these generations, the one common denominator is that they all need a place to live. So if you can take advantage of this fantastic opportunity to buy and hold for a few years, when the Millennials come into the real estate market, you will in essence have more qualified buyers and renters for any real estate properties you may be holding. WOW! This means you will have higher sales prices because of supply and demand: there will be more buyers and higher rents because there will be more renters.

With this knowledge, you can see the earnings potential you have when you "cherry pick" your wholesale real estate deals and keep the very best ones for yourself. And it is not all bad to be buying and holding properties in the wholesale real estate business. The fact that you are *also* a property owner—and not just a moneymaking dealmaker—gives you credibility with your clients. Wholesaling is also a powerful cash machine that will generate funds for your real estate deals. It is a great way to come up with down payments, to save money to purchase a home with cash, and to pay down existing debt on real estate to help increase your cash flow. Once you open your mind to the great potential of this market, the opportunities are endless.

History shows us that in any market or with any commodity, the most successful investors have made moves opposite to the prevailing market trend. That means that in a market where everyone is afraid to buy and trying to sell, the successful investor is out there buying up everything possible. When the market takes a turn up and the buying confidence is restored to the masses and the media tells them it's safe to buy, then supply and demand will come into play and prices will rise. So today's buyers will be tomorrow's greatly positioned sellers—which, if you are reading this book, will be *you* along with other savvy investors.

- Buy low and sell high -

This is the motto used in any business that involves buying and selling. The stock market traders have lived by this concept since the beginning of stock trading. Real estate is no different. We can all agree that right now the real estate market is in a downward cycle. And as with any cycle, it will eventually turn upward again. Dictionary.com defines *cycle* as: any complete round or series of occurrences that repeats or is repeated.

This book will show you some great strategies to use in the current real estate downturn to generate cash flow and increase personal holdings and net worth. As you will discover, in the real estate investing business, you are not able to buy and keep *every* good property you encounter; however, you will also have many great opportunities to make large amounts of cash rather quickly, cash that you can then invest in properties you decide to retain in your personal portfolio. In this book, I concentrate on *wholesale* and *retail* flipping. I provide insight and basic strategy on these topics, and show you how I operate my business employing these tactics.

> *I present my successful flipping principles AND I give you a view from the trenches: I show you the numbers.*

The beauty of real estate investing is that there are multiple ways to make money; there are also several pitfalls and ways to lose money. As with any market or business, many niches exist, and any new real estate investor should first find their own particular niche and stick with it until it is mastered. Once you master that niche, *then* you can safely expand into other areas. I have found several areas that are very successful, and I reveal those to you herein. I use multiple strategies to make money in this business, and if one strategy isn't working during a particular time period, for whatever reason, I employ another strategy and still turn a profit. Whatever your niche or passion, I'm sure you will get value from this book and be able to put these methods to use in your own personal real estate ventures.

Another factor plaguing this business is fear. It's hard to watch any news station and not hear something about the economy in crisis or the real estate foreclosure epidemic that is plaguing our country. Sales in most industries have slowed if not come to a halt altogether, and real estate sales have been one of the hardest hit of the entire economy. The cycling of the real estate market is an indication as to why that is. If you, the investor, can understand and grasp what is taking place and why, then you are in a great position to benefit from this and create long-lasting wealth.

Before you can understand the forces in play, you must first get yourself in the right mindset psychologically. What I'm saying is that human beings are not the rational creatures we like to believe we are. We don't always act in our own best interest. Instead of using the term "human beings," a better term might be "psychological beings." This is because we are driven more by our *primary reactions*—whether good or bad—and this can be better stated as follows:

> *We are driven most by pain or pleasure.*

As we experience extreme psychological states, they cloud our perceptions of risk and it becomes difficult for us to make good sound investment decisions. When people experience economic pleasures—during a real estate boom for instance—they are overly optimistic, and any perception or ability to assess risk dissipates quickly. On the other hand, when people experience financial pain, as in a recession, they become overly pessimistic and perceive any investment—especially in real estate—as exceedingly risky, when actually it is not.

There are theories and opinions about our current real estate market and where it is headed. Forecasts and predictions are generally useless without an explanation that gives us a viable reason for the events taking place. Unfortunately, with economics there is never a clear consensus or accepted opinion. Many "expert" economists hold that economic booms or busts are caused by external shock factors. An external shock factor, for example, can be an increase in the price of oil or new technologies hitting the marketplace. This explanation implies that there are irregular economic fluctuations. History tells us, however, that the economic boom and bust cycle is a regular phenomenon that has existed throughout time.

The problem is that there is no *one single business cycle.* There are major cycles, combined with minor ups and downs, plus small random fluctuations. So if you look at Gross Domestic Product year by year, it may look irregular, but if you look at the bigger picture, you will notice a clear cyclical pattern. The economy is like those disorganized diagrams with jumbles of lines, but there is a picture in the drawing, and if you look hard enough, you can see the cyclical pattern. And once you see it, it then seems obvious to you. Another way to gain this insight is to work in the business long enough to understand these patterns, as I have done.

Homer Hoyt, a famous real estate economist from the Great Depression, discovered an eighteen-year real estate cycle in Chicago, which coincided with the business cycles for the economy as a whole. In general, a boom precedes every depression era, and every boom is dominated by real estate. This is basically saying: *what goes up must come down*. Real estate values and the construction industry peaked just a year or two prior to the 1st Great Depression, indicating that real estate is also a cause of a downtown or bust.

Now take that thought process with what is occurring in the current real estate industry. The real estate market did not really start to bust until 2007. And then consider what happened from 2004 – 2006: values were steadily rising and the construction industry was rapidly on the rise. Then, in the last two years, values have come crashing down and the construction industry has all but come to a halt. Historically, a recession will begin soon after real estate peaks out. So if the peak occurred in 2006, and the last (minor) real estate "depression" took place in 1990, then history would indicate the next real estate depression would be in 2008. This also corresponds to the eighteen-year cycles that Homer Hoyt discovered. It is hard to argue against that result, given current economic conditions.

So if history is going to repeat itself once again, what does this information mean? As you may know, there were more millionaires created during the 1st Great Depression than any other era in history. We all know the economy has been in a financial windfall and there has been no stopping it—until now. The history of cycles implies that is must drop down before it will come back up. I don't think we are going to hit the lows of the 1st Great Depression with this current depression we are entering, mainly because the government is injecting billions of dollars into the financial system to keep it afloat. But the same opportunities will be available to the savvy investors of today as were available to the savvy investors of the 1st Great Depression. Many equity investors will get lucky by timing the stock market right, but to me that is as foolish as gambling in a casino.

Many others will make their millions investing in real estate, which some consider a gamble but many consider sound because real estate is a tangible item that we can see and touch. Unlike other investments, at the end of the day, no matter what comes of the economy, I'll still be able to have my dirt and brick property known as real estate. And let us not forget:

> No matter what is going on in the economy, or whatever the financial state of the Union, people will always need shelter.

If you are a real estate investor or if you are considering real estate investing to grow your personal wealth, you should be oozing with excitement. The investors of this 2nd Great Depression have a distinct advantage over the investors of the 1st Great Depression. We have a definite higher demand for quality housing. We are coming into the echo boom and the Millennial Generation will need housing.

All these factors in my opinion are creating the perfect storm. Think about it. We have a definite demand for housing with the growing population. Accompanied with a tightening credit market, good people losing their homes to foreclosures and bankruptcies, and the banks sitting on all these properties they have to sell but with no buyers in sight. A definite oversupply is taking place. When you consider all of these factors, you conclude there is one feasible conclusion: *now is the best time to buy as much real estate as you can.*

1 – Building Your Wholesale Team

No wholesale operation can be successful with just one person. It requires internal resources and external partners, or people in the field available to provide assistance. Below, I am listing out the various types of professionals that you should have available within your organization (on your payroll in some capacity) or that you should maintain a business relationship with so you can draw upon their services as required. The core of my team is comprised of two people that pull everything together and make the deals work. We also have other individuals and various professionals that we call upon on a regular basis.

Real Estate Licensees

We have a licensed person and an unlicensed person on our team (the two core members I'm referencing above). The real estate licensee provides our team with access to the Multiple Listing Services, board contracts, and other great tools that realtors can use to their advantage. However, they also have some restrictions. The licensee must always disclose their status as a real estate licensee to potential sellers and buyers; they are more susceptible to lawsuits from disgruntled persons when deals go awry; there are strict rules as well in most states for real estate licensees. For example, they are prohibited from marketing a property they do not own, which is a fundamental part of the wholesaling business. Be very careful if you are a wholesaler who obtains a real estate license. Always properly disclose your agent status and intentions with property. Adding a non-licensee to your team is an absolute must.

General Contractor/Estimator

Unless you can fill this position yourself, you will need to call upon a general contractor or estimator to provide an estimation of repairs. This is critical for a number of reasons. It helps build credibility with our investors, and more importantly, it helps structure wholesale fees, which are the bottom-line revenues of this business. Establishing a quality, ongoing relationship with an estimator can be tricky. If you currently do not have a good relationship with one, I suggest doing the following to establish one. Find a good one and offer to pay them for each house they evaluate and create an estimate for. If the estimator spends a couple of hours creating an estimate of the repairs, you can pay them fifty dollars or so (depending on the region of the country you are in). You can also make referrals for them to other investors, so they can pick up more business. The up-front money along with the referrals will make them happy to help you out and be accurate in their work.

Other Wholesalers

You may be wondering why you would want to include someone on your team who does the same thing as you do. The reason is to increase the buyer pool available to you. If you have a great property but no immediate buyers, another wholesaler may have a buyer for it. Rather than having a property sit, I'd rather split the fee with another wholesaler and make half the fee. Half a fee is better than no fee any day of the week.

Administrative Assistant

This is the third unnamed person on our team. Once your operation gets large enough (and believe me, if you work at it hard enough, it will), you will need someone to help out with the office and clerical tasks. Possible duties include:

- Internet advertising
- Phone calls for leads
- Paperwork

Website Administrator

Once you build your website, you will want to keep it up-to-date with basic information and a flow of new deals. There is no need to get too fancy with it, as it can consume a large amount of time. You may be able to learn some website basics yourself and keep up on it yourself once your initial site is established.

REO Realtors

These are great to have on your team because they will provide you with the good bank-owned deals as well as give you information on motivated banks and asset managers. Establishing a relationship with these realtors can be difficult. The reason for this is straightforward: In this difficult market, they are overworked and have little time for socialization.

The quickest and most reliable way to establish a working relationship with an REO realtor is to close a few deals with them in a short timeframe. After you close a deal, send them a postcard, letter, or some sort of gift card for lunch or something. Corresponding with them like this, after you have closed a deal or two, will make them remember you, and the next time a good REO property comes available, they will know who you are and how to contact you.

Title Company or Real Estate Attorney

You will need a title service that will allow you to conduct double closings and assignments. In comparing a title company and an attorney, I've had my best luck dealing with attorneys on this matter. Once you have a good title company that is closing the front and back side of your deals, you will have an advantage over your competition. Double closings are not illegal, but many inexperienced title companies will have a difficult time with anything that is not a vanilla, owner-occupied, straightforward deal. Having a legally savvy title company that can conduct a double closing for you properly—within the guidelines of the law—can make or break you as a wholesaler.

Private/Hard-Money Source

It is always good for you to provide proof-of-funds with offers and to make your front-end closings wet on your double closings. Finding a good hard-money lender is not as difficult as you might think. A lot of times you can find one—or at least a good lead for one—at a Real Estate Investor's Association (REIA) meeting or at some other local investor club meeting. I suggest getting pre-approved with one before you start wholesaling. That way you can provide proof of funds to close with cash offers, and when you do find a property that you want to buy for yourself, you are not scrambling to come up with the funds. A good hard-money lender can provide you proof of funds to close quickly; however, it will not be free. I find that most hard-money lenders charge anywhere from 4-

6 points and 13-16 percent interest on the money. Just be sure to check what other fees they try to slide into the deal. I have found that some tend to get "carried away."

2 – Structuring Your Business

Before discussing this topic, I must stress that I am not a tax professional. For sound advice, you must seek a tax professional who is familiar with your local tax laws and your personal situation. The reason I'm touching on this subject is because as a wholesale real estate investor, you may be subject to certain federal tax codes that you wouldn't otherwise be subject to. If you need clarification on any of the topics discussed in this section, please seek additional advice from a Certified Public Accountant or attorney.

When I wholesale either an REO or consumer-owned property, I always do so using my S Corporation. My tax professional (and please seek advice from yours) advised me to do this because once you accumulate a certain number of real estate transactions in a one-year period, the IRS classifies you as a real estate "dealer." As a dealer, your tax rate is not based on the capital gains rate; rather, it is based on the ordinary income rate. That means you can pay fifty percent (50%) of your hard-earned income in taxes. OUCH! By using an S Corporation, I can pay myself—as an individual—a reasonable and customary salary for running this business (and this is usually based on total sales made by our company) while taking the rest of the company's profits in the form of a *dividend*. By structuring it this way, I cut my taxes down to almost thirty-five percent (35%) on a large portion of my earnings.

Being in the real estate business, you are going to find real estate deals that you want to invest in yourself. This is one of the greatest benefits of being a wholesale investor. Not taking advantage of these opportunities would be a serious mistake. My tax professional has advised me as follows: if I hold any real estate for myself, I need to do it using a Limited

Liability Company (better known as an LLC).

A good wholesaler needs to set up at least two entities: an LLC and an S Corp. The more you grow in your business and progress, the more you will rely on the various other legal entities you may or may not need in order to efficiently transact business. For my own business, I have two S corporations and three LLCs. In a later part of this book, I'll discuss some other revenue streams that are available from your wholesaling business. These other revenue streams reinforce the need for these various business entities.

3 – The Art of Flipping

To Flip or Not to Flip

In this day and age, "flipping" has become a common household word. It seems that everyone—both real estate novice and seasoned investor—knows the basic idea of what flipping a house is. This us understandable with so many reality TV shows portraying it as an easy way to make a huge amount of money. But any experienced investor will tell you this is totally false and that these shows do not portray the harsh realities of flipping.

And now, with the recent downturn in the market and the accompanying gloom and doom from the media, flipping a home can be financial suicide. However, if you know what you are doing, there are some fantastic opportunities in the world of flipping. This is primarily because there are two different types flipping: 1) *the retail flip,* which is when you sell to a person who will be living in the home, and 2) *the wholesale investor flip,* which is when you sell the property to a landlord who is using a buy-and-hold strategy. I'm going to talk about both of these methods below and discuss the pros and cons of each.

The Retail Flip

A retail flip is the most common flip and the type most people have heard of. It is the one portrayed on all the television shows. The concept is simple and works like this: You go out and find a home in need of repair or updating. You purchase the home for 60-70 cents on the dollar. You do some renovations and add value to the property. Once the update is complete, you put the home on the market and hope to sell it for a profit of 10-20% of what the home is worth. This was not a bad way to earn a living back in the mid-2000s when homes were flying off the shelf and the lending institutions were giving anyone and everyone a loan to purchase a home. But with the tightening lending landscape, and with homes not selling as easily, this can be a very risky play.

Since a retail flip is geared towards retail buyers, meaning buyers who are going to live in the home, selling the renovated property can be a long and costly process. For example, consider the greater Cincinnati Ohio area. Back in the mid-2000s, most retail flippers were making profits of $20,000 to $30,000 per flip, with the median sales price of these homes being in the 160's. But with the recent market downturn, and with the resulting slew of homes on the market, many flippers are taking losses on their homes. This is a direct result of carrying costs and declining sales prices.

However, there is still hope for a retail flipper. I have developed a method to capitalize on the retail flip market, a sure way to make huge profits. My secret is to market to first-time homebuyers and flip homes in this price range. There are several reasons for this approach. First, interest rates are currently at an all-time-low, and first-time borrowers are able to obtain mortgages at these excellent rates. Second, first-time buyers do not have another home sitting on the market that must sell before a new one can be purchased. These buyers are often renting, so they can understand the upside in making an investment in a home, especially when they can get it at a price considered to be a bargain.

This strategy does have a certain amount of risk, but it is not significant when compared to the total investment and possible gains. Although you may not make $20,000 to $30,000 per flip, if you consider the *percentage of profit*, or your rate of return, your investment is a good one.

Here is an example of one of my recent retail flips. I purchased a foreclosed home for $34,000 cash. The home needed $15,000 in renovations to make it ready for the market. The home had a fair market value of $100,000, so I had invested a total of $49,000 into a $100,000 home, for a difference of $51,000, which is not bad. To move it quickly I priced it at $70,000 and turned a $21,000 profit. With this home, I was fortunate enough to find someone on a presale program (discussed shortly), and I closed on the home immediately upon completion of the renovations. The time from my close on the property (purchase) to the closing with my buyers (sale) was a total of 50 days. I made a $21,000 profit on my investment of 49,000 in just 50 days. On an annualized rate of return I made 312% on my money! WOW! *Where can I make more investments like that?*

There is a trick, however. In order for this type of flip to be successful, you must be willing to make some basic renovations to the home. First, you must make it stand out. I always install new windows (unless they are already vinyl), new baths, new kitchens, ceramic tile in kitchens and baths, Pergo flooring in the dinning room and living room, and new upgraded carpet in the bedrooms. The logic in this is simple. *I want to blow away any other home in my price range,* and most of these (because of the price range) are likely going to lack updates. This makes my home stand out above the rest. I want to give that first time home buyer a home they can be proud of, one that is not a "fixer upper" or in need of "TLC."

The second part of this strategy is to give your buyer some instant equity to seal the deal. In my case, I gave my buyers a 30 percent equity position of their home. Part of the selling feature of my home is that they can live in the home, which has already been totally updated, for a few years and then sell it for a profit to put down on a newer, move-up home. WOW. What an incentive. In essence, I have created a *savings plan* for their future. How cool is that? Not only am I helping them get a great home with built-in equity, I am also making a 312% rate of return on my investment. Before I go on, let me show you how I calculated my annualized rate of return on my investment:

Original investment:	**$49,000**
Profit:	**$21,000**
Time it took to make profit:	**50 days**

For annualized rate of return, use the rate of return if the money would perform at this level for a full year: 365 days per year, so that means there are 7.3 blocks of 50 days. Take the 21k profit made in 50 days and multiply by 7.3, which = $153,300. Divide that by the initial 49k investment and you have 3.12, or 312 percent.

Now let me share with you the genius of pre-selling these first-time-buyer homes. I developed a program I call "Old Homes New Beginnings." I developed the concept for this program one day when a friend asked me to help find a home for relatives of his. They were a young couple and pre-approved for $80,000. Most of my friends don't understand exactly what I do for a living. They think I'm just a realtor and that I find homes for people to live in. I have chosen not to be a realtor because of the small commissions involved. A 3% commission on an $80,000 sale works out to be $2,400. After I figure in the expense associated with the time I spend showing several homes to these first-time buyers, and after deducting the expense associated with the time I spend in the closing process, and after deducting what my managing broker takes of my commission, there just isn't very much left of that $2,400. Thanks but no thanks.

So when I talk to new and excited prospective clients, I pitch this idea: I tell them that I own a renovation company and that I purchase a lot of foreclosed homes. Most new, prospective homeowners are generally excited and they are intrigued by the thought of renovating a home because they have seen all the reality shows on TV about house flipping. I tell them I have this

"Old Homes New Beginnings" program that will benefit them. I explain that I need them to write out the five most important features they MUST HAVE in a home. Be it bedroom count, yard size, location, or whatever. I then ask them to write out the five things that they WOULD LIKE TO HAVE but that are not necessary. Usually this list includes creature comforts like central air, new windows, and ceramic tile.

I then go out and find several foreclosures that would meet their needs, and I take them to see these homes. I then show them my plans to renovate them. Now here is the clincher that makes this program so successful: *I tell them that the renovation process is very similar to the process that occurs when a person builds a brand new home.* I let them pick out some of their own paint colors, I give them a few choices on flooring and tile, and I even allow them to upgrade for additional cost. They love it! These first-time homeowners always feel like the red carpet is being rolled out for them. In all their wildest dreams, they never imagined they could get all this service and attention in the price range they are in.

To make all of this work, and to allow them to pick their own colors and flooring, I explain that they will need to put some "skin in the game." I already know that as first-time homebuyers, they are eligible for a loan on this home; I just need to make sure they have a vested interest in the deal, and that they are not going to walk away after we get started. I tell them that this program requires an "enrollment fee" of $3,000, which is nonrefundable. I have to call it an enrollment fee instead of earnest money because I do not yet own the home, so legally I cannot take their money and call it "earnest money." You cannot take earnest money for a sale on a home you do not yet own. I explain that once they buy the home from me, the enrollment fee will then become an earnest money deposit to be applied to the home's purchase price, or to their closing costs.

To make the numbers work, and to protect myself financially, I target foreclosed homes that are priced $40,000 dollars and below. I want to be sure that the required repairs can be accomplished for $20,000 or less. Now, just because I am targeting $40,000 homes does not mean I am going to pay $40,000. My goal is to be able to buy and renovate the home for no more than $50,000 total invested. I calculate the repairs on each home, which gives me my Maximum Allowable Offer (or MAO).

The reason I choose $50,000 as my price point is because it allows me multiple exit strategies. I am holding $3,000 dollars of the buyer's money, or just over 5% of my initial investment. If they walk away, I am all in for $47,000 on this $100,000 dollar home. At that point, if the deal falls through, I could stick it on the market for a new buyer or I could even make it a cash flow rental property.

At this point, my risk is very minimal, and the investment makes sense. So my program "Old Homes New Beginnings" is born.

In this market, with the slowdown of "move-up buyers" buying new homes, this type of transaction is the only type of retail flip I will do. The first-time buyers are still out there and are looking for a great home at a bargain price. With my "Old Homes New Beginnings" concept, I am able to give it to them and still make a nice profit for myself. If you follow my guidelines in your own particular marketplace, you should be able to capitalize too. Another benefit to this type of flip is the types of homes you're competing against. Remember that a lot of the baby boomers are starting to age and leave their homes of 30 or more years—homes that are in dire need of updating. Most heirs to these homes simply try to sell them as-is to settle the estate. These homes are in generally good neighborhoods but they are out of date so they get listed for a lower price, one that is in the price range of first-time buyers. If you have a first-time buyer who happens across one of these sweet old homes that needs updating, or one of your newly renovated homes, (with equity still in it), which one do you think they will tend to favor? Generally it is the freshly renovated home.

My point is simple. If you are a retail flipper who enjoys helping neighborhoods and new homeowners get a beautiful home with great equity, you can still do that and make excellent profits, even in today's market. On the other hand, if you have never flipped a home and have always wanted to try it, but the gloom and doom of today's market has you scared, then I can tell you with confidence that you can do it and still make a large profit. You just need to reprogram your though process around the idea of flipping and apply the concept of flipping for first-time buyers as I discussed above.

The Wholesale Investor Flip

With all the great deals available in today's marketplace, more and more investors—or wannabe investors—are coming out of the woodwork to get in on the action. This can present a huge opportunity for the flipper who is cash-positioned or has the backing of a good hard money source. I do more wholesale flips than any other type of deal right now. Before I go further, let me explain what a *wholesale investor flip* is. This is not an official real estate term, but something I made up to describe the process. A wholesale investor flip is a flip done with another investor, most likely a landlord who is going to use a buy-and-hold strategy. The idea here is you buy a distressed property, put enough into it to make it a nice rental—which usually requires fewer funds than what a retail flip requires—and turn it over to a buy-and-hold investor.

Your target market for this type of property is an investor who has great credit and enough funds for a down payment that is going to get conventional financing on the property. Ideally you will have developed a list of pre-qualified landlords and other investors who you can sell these to. Later, I'll discuss how to find and screen these buyers.

The advantage of wholesale investor flips, as opposed to retail flips, is that you are likely doing this flip with someone who is ready to purchase the home. In order for this process to be successful, you need to give that new landlord a great product that will produce cash flow as well as give them an instant equity position. When I do a wholesale investor flip, I give my investor a 20% cash-on-cash return as well as a 25% equity position. For those of you scratching your heads, let me tell you what a cash-on-cash return is. Simply put, it is the amount of annualized return you earn on your hard money that you put into a deal.

So let's consider an example. Suppose you purchase a home for $100,000 and the bank requires a 20% down payment, or $20,000. In order to receive a 20% cash-on-cash return on your investment, the property needs to produce an annual *positive* cash flow—which is money left over after all expenses—of $4,000. Divide the annual cash flow by 12 months and you need that property to produce $333 per month of cash flow to reach a target goal of 20% rate of return on your cash investment. Remember, this is based on the $100,000 home scenario. So I have just given you the value of a $5,000 lesson in one paragraph! Your welcome!

Now that you know how to calculate a cash-on-cash return, let me take you back a step. If you can deliver a 20% cash-on-cash return to an investor AND also give them a 20%-25% equity position in a freshly rehabbed property, if it is a serious investor, you will likely make the sale. I give my investors additional comfort by explaining my process of a rehab and how I am trying to make the property maintenance free (with the exception of bad tenants) for 5 years. I also go a step further and warranty all my rehab work for 12 months. Chances are, there will not be many callbacks on your rehab in the first 12 months if you do it right. This warranty is something you can offer to these newer investors to keep them coming to you.

Let's consider the numbers on a wholesale investor flip I recently completed. I purchased a foreclosed home in a C+ rental neighborhood for $22,000 cash from the bank. The home was in decent shape and only required $13,000 cash in renovations to make it an excellent rental. Once we completed the rehab, which took 5 weeks, we had $35,000 invested in a 4-bedroom, 1-bath home, which was worth approximately $70,000. The home had a rental market value of $825 per month. I sold this home to an investor—I had it pre-sold before we even closed with the bank—for $48,000, giving me a $13,000 profit in just 38 days, which was the timeframe from close to close. So in my numbers, I made an annualized rate of return on my money of 356% (see above example for how this is calculated). More importantly, let's look at my buyer's numbers.

He paid $48,000 for a home valued at $70,000, giving him an instant equity position of 31% in the property. He made a down payment of 20%, which translates into $9,600 out of pocket cash. With the rent of $825 per month, after expenses he had a positive monthly cash flow of $300 per month. So, for a cash-on-cash return, his rate is 37.5%. WOW. Not bad, huh? Given these numbers, I probably should have charged more for this property; however, my theory is if they are getting good deals from me that they can't get anywhere else, that translates to more sales and business for me in the future. This particular client buys about 3-5 properties from me per quarter, each of them generating similar numbers as outlined on the above deal. If you figure out the math, you can see how much we are making. (I'll save you the trouble: in one quarter, he increases his equity position by roughly $88,000 and he increases his positive cash flow by $1,200 per month. So, hypothetically, if we start January 1, at the end of March, his real estate investment portfolio has increased by $88,000 and his monthly income is $1,200 a month more than it was on January 1st. At the end of December, his portfolio has increased by $352,000 and his monthly income is $4,800 a month more than it was on January 1st. If we continue doing this for 5 years, at the end of that period, $1.76 million in equity has been added to his portfolio (not accounting for other factors) and his monthly income has increased by $24,000.) The amount of money you can make is astounding.

I recently had a property manager tell me that she has no problem filling the vacancies and renting up the properties that we rehab. She explained that investors who are bringing her the renovated properties of ours are renting to the first people who view them. She also understands that the maintenance required on our properties will be minimal because of the quality of rehab that we do.

The point I'm making is this: We go into the wholesale investor flip with a similar mentality as the retail flip. We have discovered that there are more renters—and better quality renters—coming back into the current rental marketplace. In a lot of these C-grade neighborhoods, a lot of homes are for rent. The good news is most of them will not be of the quality and/or freshness as one of our rent-ready rehabs. We want to attract a better quality tenant base as well as retain the property when a lease turns over. If the property is one of the nicest homes in the area for rent, and the rents we charge are comparable, then it is easy to see which home is going to rent—ours! So, to be successful, it pays to give a good quality rehab.

I always include the following in my rehabs:

- Ceramic tile in kitchen and baths
- New furnace if current furnace is more than 8 years old and it is not high efficiency
- Central air if not present
- New vinyl windows if not present
- New water heater if older than 4 years
- Replace any suspicious plumbing with new PVC
- Glass block all basement windows
- Whitewash paint all basements
- New countertops and cabinets in kitchens
- New bathroom fixtures
- New carpet in all bedrooms
- Some type of Pergo or laminate flooring in common areas and hallways
- Fresh neutral paint throughout the home

If the owner of the property on the back side of the deal does not want these items completed, or if I'm being general contracted out and they don't want to pay for these, then I won't do them. But this is what goes into 95% or more of our rehabs.

The home rents faster because it looks newer and fresher and it has nicer amenities. Also, from a maintenance perspective, I've discovered that ceramic tile will hold up longer than any peel-and-stick floor available. When the tenant moves out, chances are a peel-and-stick flooring will be damaged; however, your ceramic will be in good condition. I've also come to realize that a new furnace and windows are necessary in cold climates of the country. Sure, the old ones may still work, but they will cost your tenant dearly. Most investors would say, "Well that's their problem and not mine," but they are dead wrong; it *is* the investor's problem. If the heating bill is too exorbitant, the tenant will not have enough money to pay the rent. OUCH!

On the other hand, if they pay the rent and do not run enough heat then the plumbing will freeze? OUCH again! So the best thing for everyone is to make sure the tenant can afford the winter heating bill. A new water heater ensures happy tenants are not running out of hot water in the middle of a shower and the central air ensures they are not miserable from the heat. It all makes sense after you do it for a while.

If you chose to do investor flips, be sure to have enough money to cover the above items so you can keep everyone happy. Once you work out the rehab numbers required to cover these expenses, you will have your Maximum Allowable Offer (MAO, See Appendix). You then know the top offer you can make on a property you have identified for this type of investment.

If you are going to flip property, I recommend doing a blend of retail and wholesale investor flips. I concentrate more on the wholesale flip right now because that is what the market is commanding; however, I do like my retail first time buyer flips. My personal investing rules allow me to do one retail flip per quarter and as many investor wholesale flips as I possibly can.

4 – How to Find Deals

Finding good deals is almost an art, but many of the ingredients that lead to success are related to hard work and due diligence. I can reveal several methods that consistently work for me, but in the end, you will discover other methods that fit your own personal style and supplement these sure-fire techniques.

Renovation Costs

Let me first say that if you are going to find wholesale deals that are in need of renovations—and most of them are—then you need to learn how to estimate the renovations accurately or find someone you can partner with to help you with this. And this is why: nothing aggravates me, as an investor, more than being sent a wholesale deal with estimated renovations of $15,000. On paper, the deal looks good, so I go and look at it personally, but when I get there, right away I can see that the renovations are going to be $35,000 or so. How many times am I going to look at this wholesaler's deals if he keeps underestimating the renovations? I understand that it is sometimes difficult to accurately estimate renovations. So in all my deals I include a list of general large ticket items that are in my "Estimation of Renovations."

When I package a deal, you will see something like this at the bottom:

Suggested renovations:

- New vinyl windows
- New furnace
- Paint/patch
- New flooring
- Ceramic tile in kitchen and bath
- New bathroom fixtures
- Gutter repair

I do this so an investor can see exactly how I determined my numbers. He or she can then say, "Well, I'll leave the wood windows in and save some money," or "I may be able to save money on the furnace because Uncle Joe is a furnace guy and he owes me a favor." You will build credibility with investors when you can show them how you determined your renovation numbers and let them be realistic in what the home needs based on the list you provided. I suggest getting a Cost Book at a hardware store. It will give you a general idea of what repairs costs.

Finding the Deals

There are many ways to find wholesale deals. There are so many, in fact, that it is not possible to cover all of them in this book, so I'm going to talk about the best ones that I use and a couple others that you may also want to consider. A lot of information on this subject is available, online and off, if one of my methods does not suit you or your style.

The MLS Shotgun Method

This is by far my favorite and most successful. I use this to come up with 90% or more of my deal flow. It is easy for me because I am a licensed real estate broker in the states I work in. If you are not a licensed broker, but you still want to use this method, then I would suggest either adding a good realtor to your team or getting a license yourself.

Here is how I do it. I search the MLS daily and even auto-prospect using the MLS as my tool and I target my sub-markets. Depending on the sub-market and what my needs are, I'll filter the results. For example, in the Price Hill sub-market, I target single-family, four-bedroom homes. These seem to yield the most spread. I also watch for duplex homes that can be converted to four-bedroom, single-family homes. I pull up the active listings, and I write contracts on these properties. I don't go inside them or even drive by. I'm looking for motivated sellers that need to dump their properties. I usually just start by offering 45% percent of list price.

I have systemized this approach somewhat to make it easier than it sounds. Our local board contract is six pages. In addition to that, all offers require a copy of an earnest money check, agency disclosure, and proof of funds (which I'll discuss later). The only new page I create before I send over a contract is page 1 for a given day. So if I'm writing ten offers on Monday the first, then all ten of those offers have the same closing date, same inspection times, etc. I then generate a new page one that has address and price for each property. To be successful with this shotgun approach, you need to make at least fifty offers per week because you are not going to get them all; you are playing the "law of large numbers" to find some exceptional deals suitable for wholesaling.

When you consider the amount of time spent, using the MLS offers several advantages. It allows you to search by neighborhood and reveal the properties that are available right now. The *length of time on market* is also visible for these properties, and you can use that to your advantage. I like to target bank-owned homes that have been on the market at least thirty days or more.

Driving for Dollars Method

The name says it all. You literally drive around your target sub-markets one to two times per week (or more depending on your sub-market size, turn rate, etc.) and gather phone numbers for all properties that have For Sale By Owner (FBSO) or For Rent signs. And then you simply call them. Ask a few screening questions and see if you can make a deal. This is a great way to generate short sale and subject-to deals. Obviously, this method is very time consuming, and there are travel expenses involved. I suggest hiring a "bird dog" for this tactic. If this person brings you a good lead and you make a profit from the deal, then you give them a piece of the earnings. I generally pay my bird dogs $500 per successful close. If the deal is really good and I make more, then I'll give them $1,000.

Here are some possible screening questions:

- Why are you selling your property? (You are looking for a motivated seller who is selling because the *have* *to* (foreclosure, estate liquidation, etc.), not because they *want to.*
- How much do you owe on your home?
- What repairs does it need?
- What is it worth?
- How much of an offer in cash could you accept today?

All of these questions will reveal information that will improve your ability to make a decision.

Evictions List Method

Most landlords are fed up with a property just after evicting a tenant. They are upset about the loss of income they have just experienced. To top it off, they just spent hundreds of dollars evicting the tenant, and now, when they finally get their property back, they have to go in and spend excessive amounts of money bringing it back into a rentable condition. Then they have to go through the trouble of taking applications, screening tenants, etc. When an investor offers them a quick easy solution to unload their troubled property, they will be a captive audience to whatever you have to say. I don't suggest this as a primary lead source; however, I do suggest that you keep this one in your arsenal and put it to use when you are deal searching and you notice one of these. Most of the court dockets for evictions are public record, so you can pick them up. If you have the time, find out when eviction court is in session, and show up there. You can meet the landlords outside, and hand out some business cards and introduce yourself. You may have to do this a few times before they warm up to you, but eventually it can pay off significantly.

Summary

There are several methods to find deals. The above are just a few that I have had success with. I recommend researching other methods, or you can just get out there and try different things and see what works best for you. Personally, I've tried several methods and the MLS (Multiple Listing Shotgun) is the best one. With that approach, I find the most productive deals, and I have almost instantaneous results.

5 – Pricing Deals

Pricing is one of the most important aspects of your wholesaling business. The process of determining price can be very tricky because it is affected by geographic location. The ideas and principals in Cincinnati OH—where the median price on a single family home is currently $160,000—do not necessarily apply to and a similar home in San Francisco—where the median pricing of that home is $800,000. Pricing varies from region to region. Wholesale fees are also a function of the market. When your dealing with higher end properties in more expensive markets, then your fees are generally going to be higher than they would be in lower priced markets, such as Cincinnati Ohio.

How to Price Your Deals

In today's highly depressed market, I like to give my investors a great equity position so the deal is "too good to pass up." I put them into the deal at no more than 65% of the After Repaired Valued (ARV). What does that mean? We can illustrate the concept with a $100,000 property example:

Location:	Cincinnati, OH
Description:	4-bdrm, 2-bath
Purchase Price:	$40,000
Estimated Renovations:	$25,000
After Repair Value:	$100,000

The total investment is Purchase Price + Estimated Renovations, or $65,000. After Repair Value is $100,000, and 65% of the ARV is the total investment or the offer amount of 65,000.00. Easy enough, right?

If your particular market allows you to price deals higher than 65% of ARV, then great; it means more money for you. On the other hand, if you are in a highly competitive market, you may want to consider going below the 65% threshold. Your market research will dictate your particular percentage and your offer amounts.

You are probably wondering how you can find out what others in your market are doing so you can get a good understanding about what percentage you should apply to your ARVs. Two great sources for finding other wholesalers in your area and seeing how they price deals are 1) Craig's list (www.craigslist.org) and 2) local Real Estate Investor Clubs, like R.E.I.A. or whatever you may have in your locality. I suggest checking these clubs out to see how they are pricing deals, but you should also pay attention to what is selling in your local market.

How do you get paid and how much do you offer for a property?
These are the million-dollar questions (well, at least thousand dollar questions!). First, you need to put a dollar value on your time and energy.

You also must determine how much money you want to make on each deal. Using the example above, if you are buying a property for $40,000—remember, you are not making money on the expenses to renovate; rather, you are making money on the purchase—and you decide that you want to make a $6,000 wholesale fee, the Maximum Allowable Offer (MAO) on that property is $34,000.

But before you make that offer, stop right there. Just because $34,000 is the most you can pay for a property doesn't mean you have to pay that amount. If you can get that property for $32,000, then you just increased your wholesale fee from $6,000 to $8,000. See how that works? Pretty simple, huh?

To sum it up, you need to determine the following:

1) The wholesale fee – How much you want to make on each deal.

2) The expected renovation costs – Be realistic, because if these are too low (and you get a higher wholesale fee), you will lose credibility with your investors very quickly. Then your business will suffer drastically (and may even fail).
3) The ARV to sell the deal at.
4) Package the deal with all the relevant information

What information do I need in a wholesale deal?
This is an interesting question with no clear-cut answer. My partner sometimes accuses me of giving "too much information on a deal," but I believe there is no such thing. I will give you some examples of how I package my information for a particular deal. The information I provide depends on the type of deal I am selling. (Note: see Appendix for a definition of these acronyms)

Example 1 – *The "buy and hold for rental deal"*

These are my bread and butter deals in this market; therefore, I know this type of investment inside and out. Here is an example of what this type of deal might look like:

Location:	Cincinnati, OH
Description:	4-bdrm, 2-bath
Purchase Price:	$30,000
Estimated Renovations:	$22,000
Estimated After Repair Value*:	$80,000

* Based on the following MLS comps, all located within a .25-mile radius in the last 6 months. All comps are comparable in size, age and amenities:

Address	DOM	SP	SD
345 Main	48	$79,000	07/24/08
567 Cross	76	$84,000	08/28/08
249 Lost	65	$82,000	08/19/08

Estimated Monthly Rental Value:	$825
Estimated Monthly Expenses:	$235
Net Operating Income (NOI):	$590
Cap Rate:	14%
Rent Factor:	.0156

Description: 123 Main was built in 1945, and according to tax records, it has a livable square footage of 1,698. Home is brick and the neighborhood grade is C+.
Contact: My information with phone number, email and website

Notice that I use terms *"Estimated* After Repaired Value" and *"Estimated* Renovations." The reason I use the word *Estimated* is as follows: Unless you are a licensed appraiser and you can guarantee that the value is what you say it is going to be, then use the word *Estimated* because you cannot guarantee the amount. By using "estimated" you are merely making it your *opinion.* You can validate your opinion with comps and an explanation of those comps. But I urge you to never guarantee anything because if and when you are wrong, it will create trouble for you in a business sense, and maybe even in a legal sense.

When Pricing my buy-and-holds for investors who are looking for these types of deals, I like to personally put them in a situation where the Rent Factor is at least .015 or greater. Rent factor is a handy figure that describes that percentage of the investment in terms of the monthly rent. For example, suppose an investor has a total of $100,000 invested in a property (this includes purchase + renovations). If it rents for $1,500 per month, it has a Rent Factor of .015.

Example 2 – *Yorkridge Analysis*

Location:	Mt. Healthy, OH
Description:	Single family 3-bdrm, 1-bath

Purchase Price:	$33,000
Estimated Renovations:	$6,000
Down Payment:	$6,600
Total Out of Pocket:	$12,900
Debt Carried:	$26,400
Loan Payment (per Month):	$158
Estimated Market Rental Value (per Month):	$800
Monthly Net Operating Income:	$332
Annual Net Operating Income:	$3,984
Cash on Cash Return:	31%

Expense Breakdown

Item	Monthly	Yearly
Debt Service:	$158.28	$1,899.36
Maintenance:	$80.00	$960.00
Vacancy:	$80.00	$960.00
Taxes:	$100.00	$1200.00
Insurance:	$50.00	$600.00
Totals:	$468.28	$5.619.36

Example 3 – *Connecticut College Hill*

Location:	Connecticut College Hill, OH
Description:	Single family, 4-bdrm, 1-bath
Purchase Price:	$20,000
Estimated Renovations:	$10,000
Estimated Market Rental Value:	$900
Estimated After Repair Value*:	$124,469
Monthly Net Operating Income:	$345
Annual Net Operating Income:	$4140
Equity Gained:	$94,469

* Based on the following MLS comps, all located within a .25-mile radius in the last 6 months. All comps are comparable in size, age and amenities:

Comps

Address	DOM	SP	SD
6014 Connecticut	57	$109,900	08/20/08
5940 Monticello	83	$117,500	10/09/08
2043 Bluebell	44	$126,575	08/29/08
1945 Connecticut	4	$143,900	06/27/08

Expense Breakdown

Item	Monthly	Yearly
Debt Service:	$214.93	$2,579.16
Maintenance:	$90.00	$1,080.00
Vacancy:	$90.00	$1,080.00
Taxes:	$100.00	$1,200.00
Insurance:	$60.00	$720.00
Totals:	$554.93	$6,659.16

6 – Handling Buyer Objections

First let me point out that if you have to handle too many objections from a particular buyer, chances are they are just a "tire kicker" and not serious. They are just wasting your time anyway.

If it's such a good deal why don't you buy it yourself?
This is a classic question that arises most often with inexperienced investors or investors who are new to your business. My response is quite simple and to the point: I tell them if I were personally able to buy each and every deal I came across, then I wouldn't be talking to them. I point out that I *do* invest in some properties and I do like to take deals for myself from time to time; however, I do not have an endless supply of funds so it is impossible for me to participate in every opportunity. I explain that in this market, there are a large number of good deals out there and

since I do this full time I find more than I can keep for myself. So if I can pass the deal off to someone else and still make five thousand or so in wholesale fees, then everybody is a winner as long as the deal works for the buyer.

Well, if you're not doing anything, then why are you making 5,000 dollars?
If you get this objection, then chances are the investor you're working with is as green as the warm summer grass, and you may not want to do business with them. I usually explain it to them one time, and if they continue to bring it up or make an issue over it, then I won't do business with them at all. I simply remind them that if the deal works for them—if their personal numbers work, and they are getting a great deal with cash flow and equity—they shouldn't care if I make $5,000 or $500,000, *as long as it works for them.* If they are not able to understand this, and are upset by the fact that I am making money on a property, then they are not seasoned investors, and chances are they

ultimately won't pull the trigger on the deal anyway. My advice to you—learned the hard way from many years of experience—is to get away from these people and don't waste your time.

Isn't this considered flipping and isn't flipping illegal?
This is a common question from realtors. There is a general misconception that flipping is illegal, and although I'm not a lawyer nor am I offering any kind of legal advice, I can tell you from my experience that flipping is NOT illegal. What *is* illegal is falsified loan documents and falsified appraisals. Because these practices were commonly used during the period when flipping was popular, they created a bad stigma around flipping and this led to the misconception that flipping is illegal. The act of flipping is legal as long as the value in the property is substantiated by valid appraisals. So when this objection surfaces, I usually state what I stated above, and that should satisfy most people. If they cannot understand it,

then it is time to move on and quit wasting time with someone who ultimately will not close the deal anyway.

Can I have an inspection period?
This is pretty common from newer people that have never worked with a wholesaler. It is important that they understand that working with a wholesaler is not the same as working on a traditional real estate deal with a realtor. In a traditional deal buyers are used to locking up a deal and having seven to ten days to inspect the property as well as having a financing contingency (see next objection). The problem with an inspection contingency is that you may have the property locked up with a bank or some other seller for only seven to ten days, and if you have an inspection period for the same time frame, then you can encounter serious problems. This great deal that you have worked so hard to put together may fall through. I tell all my buyers to complete their inspections *beforehand*, and once they pay the assignment fee for a

property, it acts as a non-refundable deposit, so I will not return the funds unless there is a title issue with the property and the seller can't close. This will also instill a sense of urgency. If you have a great property in a desirable area, they will not want to lose out and will get through the property and finish their inspections quickly.

I need to obtain a loan for this property, and it can take thirty days to close.
If your buyer is telling you that he needs to get traditional financing, then I hate to be the bearer of bad news, but you cannot work with him. This is because you may not have enough time to get financing for your initial contract with the bank. If you wrote your initial offer for cash, and now your buyer wants to finance it through an institution, you will not be able to consummate the deal because of time and contract restraints. I am aware that not everyone is sitting around with $40,000-$50,000 to put into a property; however, there are ways to come up with the funds to close

within seven to ten days. If your buyer does not have the necessary funds, then they should get approved for a private, hard-money loan first—before they start looking at any of your deals. Most hard-money deals can be put together in just five to seven days depending on whether your buyer is already set up with a lender or not. In the section titled "Building Your Wholesale Team," I suggest hooking up with a good hard-money lender. If you can develop a relationship and send them a steady flow of good buyers and profitable deals, chances are they will take care of you and possibly even send you some referral funds for the steady business you are sending them.

7 – A View From the Trenches

In this section, I'm going to tell you a little bit about how things are on the front lines of the real estate investor business. I'm going to take you along with me on some of my deals. Hopefully, this will give you more insight into the process of how I make huge profits.

The Government Bailout

When the government announced its bailout package to the country, the implication was that the government would be buying up a lot of homes that are in the foreclosure process and reselling them in the near future. A good friend of mine (who is an insider with Fannie Mae) told me that all the government agencies are expecting their current inventory of REO homes to double in the next year.

If the current agencies—HUD, Fannie Mae, and Freddie Mac—are just barely able to manage the inventory of homes they have, then how are they going to handle a surge in their home inventory next year? There are only a couple of solutions: They can hire more personnel—for an unknown amount of time—to manage these properties, all the while paying salaries and benefits to this increased staff. But the smarter move, business-wise, would be to slash prices on the current inventory and attempt to purge it.

To gain insight into any possible future trends, I watch the multiple listing service activity to see 1) if the government agencies are making price cuts, 2) if the price cuts are large, and 3) at what number of *days-on-market* they are making them. This leads into the next two case studies.

The Connecticut College Hill House

This is a great house on a cul-de-sac in an excellent neighborhood (see above for a breakdown of the deal numbers). I'm not sure why the previous owners lost the home; however, it was currently on the market and being sold by HUD. HUD is one of my favorite government agencies because they take the negative human factors out of any negotiations so it is much easier to culminate a business transaction with them. With HUD, you bid using a computer and a secure website. Everything is percentage-based and every so often, a HUD employee reduces the price of the home. The trick is anticipating these drops and being ready when they are going to do it.

By watching the MLS activity, I calculated that HUD was reducing prices on the bailout homes first at the 90-day mark and then again around the 120-140 day mark. Before the bailout, you could expect reductions of up to 30% off list price. But things were different in the bailout world.

The first reduction on the Connecticut house was from $105,000 to $63,000. Seeing such a drastic price cut means the seller is desperately trying to move this home. Once the home hit 140 days-on-market, I posted an offer of $25,000 and got rejected. Two days later, I resubmitted the offer for $20,000 and it was accepted. Even with the depressed state of the market, this is one of the best deals I have made in quite a while on a single-family home. You might be thinking: *of course the prices are going down; this is the biggest real estate failure in the history of mankind,* but remember: All markets are cyclical, and the best time to buy is during times when fear is at its highest and everyone is selling, so I view this as simply another excellent time to put money to work. It may be scary for your typical investor, but I know from experience that now is the time to strike.

So why did they reject my first offer? There is no clear reason. It just taught me to be persistent and keep trying because with HUD, you are dealing with a person who is looking at a computer screen and simply clicking *Accept* or *Reject*—the process is totally dehumanized with no emotions. A few days later, ten new houses popped up on the market in that same HUD district. It is possible that the increase in inventory caused my bid to be accepted.

The Ann Street Project

This home was another foreclosure being sold by Fannie Mae. It is located in a neighborhood that is primarily composed of rental properties. When it originally hit the market, it was listed for $29,900. This area is one of my favorite target areas, so I started watching it when it was listed. Around day 90, Fannie Mae dropped the price $5,000 to $24,900. I continued watching, hoping to get the house for around $10,000. Several days passed, and Fannie Mae dropped the price down to $14,900. I offered $8,000 at this time, and my offer was rejected.

So I let the house sit a while longer. On day 156, the bank dropped the price to $9,900. That same week, the government had finalized its bailout package of the banks. Reasoning that they were going to start dropping prices drastically to avoid the overhead associated with the personnel required to manage their additional inventory of homes, I put my theory to the test and offered $3,000. They took my offer without even countering it! That was a 70% discount from price or a 90% discount from the original list price. This was huge.

The Valley House

This home was being sold by a living, breathing human being and not a government agency. It is located in a neighborhood comprised primarily of rental property with some homeowners. This house is in a more desirable pocket of the neighborhood; however, it is situated down in a valley and you have to literally walk down 50 or so steps to get to it (hence the name, valley house). I found this house using my *driving for dollars* method and called the phone number on the For Sale by Owner Sign.

The owner told me that he bought this house when he was single and had just recently married. He indicated that his new bride did not care for the home in that neighborhood and wanted to buy a home outside the city. He had a small mortgage payment of under $3,000 per month and owed somewhere in the mid 30's on the mortgage. The home had a rental market value of $850 per month and was worth about $60,000 according to current market conditions.

I viewed the home and notified the owner of various repairs required to make it rent-ready. As we talked, he seemed to get more comfortable and he told me the real reason he was selling his home: he was tired of making the monthly mortgage payment and he just wanted to be done with the home. He was willing to sell it for what he owed on it and give someone else his equity. He didn't tell me, but possibly he was also concerned some about the current market downturn and worried that he would end up owing more than it was worth as the value plunged further. I saw an immediate opportunity: Take the home subject to the existing mortgage. I asked him questions about his monthly payment, what he owed, and other important questions for this type of deal. Once I had all the information I put an offer together I felt would be good for all of us.

My offer was to buy the house subject to existing financing. I explained that I would make the loan payments but the loan would remain in his name, and some other details. He had a few questions, but in the end he was OK with it. I then pushed a little further and told him I needed him to give me $3,000 for repairs. Not only was I asking him to deed his house over to me and leave the mortgage in his name, I was in essence asking him to pay me $3,000 to take his house. Note that it is customary in these types of deals for the buyer to pay some cash for the equity in the home. Faced with more mortgage payments coming up and not having any prospects to buy his home in the slow market, he was OK with it and agreed to take it.

I sold the home within 48 hours for a $9,000 profit. From start to finish, I spent less than 3 days on the entire deal. The new owner was happy to be in a property with great cash flow (because the mortgage was in place) and the original seller was very happy not to be making any more payments. Since I am not a greedy person, I turned the $3,000 repair credit over to the new owner and did not pocket it for myself. That way everyone was happy.

8 – Hard Money and Private Money

With conventional lending institutions growing tighter and tighter with their funds, securing appropriate funding for properties in need of rehab is becoming increasingly difficult. For this reason, hard money or private money can be your funding vehicle to get these deals done and make huge profits.

Hard Money

Before I go further, let me first tell you what hard money is. Hard money refers to funds provided by a private company or individual with cash on hand. They lend this money out, usually for a fee, based on their lending criteria for the property. There are several advantages to using hard money over traditional financing. First of all, it is usually much quicker to get the funds required to close. Most hard-money lenders are able to close in two weeks or less. Second, unlike conventional lending institutions, hard-money lenders will lend on properties that are distressed and in need of repairs. Third, they will lend you money based on a property's *after repaired value*, which is what the property will be worth when it is back in retail condition. Fourth, unlike conventional lending institutions, hard-money lenders will lend you the funds to purchase the property *and* the additional funds to renovate the property. Lastly, once you develop a relationship with your hard-money lender, you should be able to secure an open line to use like private cash.

There are a few things to be cautious of when dealing with hard money. Hard money loans are designed to be short-term loans; therefore, you can expect a balloon payment to kick in usually within six to twelve months. Since the hard-money lender is lending out their hard cash, they want to recoup it so they can put it to work again for themselves in another loan. Another thing to be aware of is the interest payment. Like I said, since this is a short-term loan, the hard-money lender wants to make a profit on the investment of the loan. Usually the points you pay, along with the hiked up double-digit interest rate for the short term, makes it worthwhile. The high interest rate is to motivate you, the borrower, to either refinance the property or sell it as soon as possible to save you the monthly interest payments. However, don't let these things stop you from using hard money; just be aware of them when exploring the differences between various hard-money lenders. Personally, I recommend that you find a hard-money lender who charges no more than five points with a 16% interest rate and, at a minimum, a six-month balloon payment on the loan. Also, check their charges for appraisals and trip fees for construction draws. You can expect these fees to be in the several-hundred-dollar range, but any more than that and

I would suggest shopping for a new lender.

From this discussion, you can see how hard-money lenders play an important role in your real estate investing. If you are wholesaling REO properties, you may need hard money to close the front end of your transactions. If you want to flip a property to investors or retail flip to homeowners, you can use hard money to get your project completed. The more the traditional banks tighten up and do away with construction loans and lending on distressed properties, the more important your relationship(s) with hard-money lenders will become.

Most hard-money lenders have mechanisms in place to protect themselves and their cash. If they do not, they will not last in this business very long. So you will likely have some hoops to jump through in order to secure the financing. For example, they will perform a credit check on you, verify the property values, and have you put some "skin in the game" in the form of points and other costs. If you decide to use hard money (and almost everyone in this business does), just remember to add the associated costs to your expenses.

In my own hard-money business, I will not lend out over 65% of the After Repaired Value (or ARV, which is the value of a property after repairs and renovations) on a particular property. What that means is if a property has an ARV of $100,000, I will not lend out more than a total of $65,000. To protect myself, I need to ensure that the comparable properties (comps) used to determine the ARV are legitimate comps, and I also make the borrower have an appraisal done on the property. I charge 5 points for the loan—a point is one percent—as well as 15% amortized over 30 years, with a 1-year balloon. I've found that my rates are about the same as other hard-money lenders I've done business with. I am by far not the "cheapest" hard-money lender available.

The reason I'm giving my rates is to tell you where I'm at in *my* pricing. This will give you an idea of how you can compare hard-money lenders that you may be considering.

Private Money

Chances are you already know someone who is a private-money lender or at least has the potential to be a private-money lender. Any person with an under performing 401K, IRA, or some other form of investment is the ideal person to become a private-money lender. Most private-money lenders are not real estate investors, they are just ordinary people that are tired of losing money in their retirement investments and want to turn it around. Personally, I pay my private money investors a 10% rate annually, paid out on quarterly dividends. With the current depressed state of the stock market and banking, how many people do you know who are earning a consistent 10%? Odds are not very many; therefore, this makes almost anyone you know a viable candidate to become a private-money lender.

One of the biggest differences between private money and hard money is private money is usually lent to a business on what is called a promissory note, which is a note that makes a promise to pay back-loaned money within an allotted amount of time and at a specified interest rate. On the other hand, hard money is a loan on a specified property, much like a conventional lender would make, with the lenders being secured in first lien position. This is difficult to accomplish with private money. Suppose that you have two different individuals giving you $25,000 each on promissory note money, and the deal you are using their funds for is a $50,000 deal. It would impossible to give both of them first lien position on the same property. The key thing a private-money lender must understand is that they are investing in your real estate business on a whole and not in one specified piece of property. Once you complete a couple successful promissory note loans, you will be able to pick up more than you need based on referrals and reputation.

Whichever source of funds you make available to yourself—either hard money or private money—be sure to secure the funds and maintain your relationship with that person or business. The wholesale real estate business—dealing with distressed properties—is becoming a cash business, and we all know that cash is king in this business.

9 – Building Your Database

Your Buyers Database

A buyers database is one of the most important assets any wholesaler can have. In reality, this is one of the most important assets that ANY businessperson can have. Building one can be a slow process in the beginning, but it is a critical component to making sales on the great deals you will find as your business grows. There are two schools of thought with respect to building a buyers database. There is the law of large numbers, which simply states that you must get as many people as possible into your database. That way when you advertise a deal to your database, hopefully one of the people behind the many email addresses will respond. Depending on the size of your database, this may be semi-successful.

Another strategy is to pre-screen and pre-qualify your buyers before you allow them onto your list. By doing this, you will have fewer names in the database; however, you will have taken the time to familiarize yourself with your clients and understand what they want. You might provide a mini-application that prospective buyers fill out. This way, you can determine what they are looking for, if they are cash buyers, and what kind of investing experience they have.

There are several ways to do this. One of the fastest is to find a great deal. Once you have your pack finished up and you're ready to market the deal, start advertising it on craigslist.org, in newspapers, and with REIA clubs. Make sure the people who respond know that you are a wholesaler and that you are constantly finding good deals. Once you obtain their personal information, add it into your database. If you encounter people who won't fill out your application or give you their information, don't worry. Add them into a secondary database with whatever information you have. Those people who take the time to fill out your application should be entered into your primary database. Let those members of your primary database see the deals first. You can also maintain a hierarchy of "classes" within your database, with the best buyers grouped into a certain class. When you find a person who consistently closes deals, move them up to a better class of buyers. Perhaps you have a class of buyers that you call first, another that you call second, and so forth, until you get a great deal under contract.

You can also use other wholesalers to build your database. When you find a great deal, offer to split the fees with them. If they market the deal to people in their database, take anyone that responds and capture their information; add them into your database. If the other wholesaler is savvy, he or she may not allow you to have contact with buyers on their list. They will keep all responses and filter them to you. In this case, you will not be able to absorb this wholesaler's database. However, once you get someone who wants to close, you will capture their information for the contract and you can still add that buyer—and it is a good addition to your database because they are serious enough to pull the trigger on deals.

Craigslist.org

I mentioned advertising your deal on www.craigslist.org. If you are not familiar with craigslist.org, you should get to know it very fast. First of all, it is the best advertising money you will ever spend: it is absolutely free! Second, there are a lot of professionals in the real estate investment community who use the forums on craigslist.org. Don't just advertise your deal in the craigslist room for your city; advertise it in all the cities that are adjacent or nearby your city. Just be prepared for out of state responses. You also may have to repost your property several times a day. This is the most effective form of Internet advertising that I have ever used.

Investor Clubs

Going to your local real estate investor club meetings is a great way to meet buyers. You will likely have to become a "vendor member" before you are allowed to market your properties. If they do not have such a requirement, you can just show up and hand out your deal flyers and your contact information. Collect all the business cards you can. People at these gatherings love to hand out cards. Add their information to your database. Just be cautious because many people at these clubs are tire kickers and seminar junkies. But if you talk to enough of them, you can play the law of large numbers for your database. Besides, they may not be the one that buys your property but they may know someone else who will buy your property. So just keep at it and build your database and you will soon see results.

Public Records

Another great resource I've used is the public records system (online and at the courthouse). Once you get a deal under contract, check the local tax records for owners who have rental property in the area. It is fairly easy to determine who these people are. Just compare the names on the mailing address for the tax records to the address of the property. If they don't match up, then you have an investor for your database. Send them a post card saying that you have a property near one of theirs for sale with the address of the deal property and your contact information. When they contact you, capture their information for that deal and possibly other deals you may get in the area. If you don't want to sift through the tax records, you can find services that sell such lists, such as Melissadata.com.

Sheriff's Sale

A great buyer-finding tool that often goes untapped is Sheriff's Sale records. Think about it for a moment. If you have never attended a Sheriff's Sale, then I suggest you go to one. If you have been to one, then you probably already know that you have to be a cash buyer and that you buy a property as is where is. These types of buyers are a wholesaler's dream. So I suggest that you find out when and where in your county (and in your neighboring county) the Sheriff's Sale takes place. Show up with your property flyer and hand it out. Once you do this a few times, the buyers will get to know you and the types of deals you have. Then you may pick up some great cash buyers for your database. If multiple sales are taking place at the same time, hire an intern or get your partner to go along as well. This way you can cover more ground and gather more cash buyers.

All and all there are many ways to develop your buyers database, and these are some solid methods that have worked best for me. The deeper into this business you go, the more advanced you will become at building your list, and the more techniques you will develop and employ.

10 – Wholesaling and REO Properties

I am constantly learning in this area because I find most of my deals by using the MLS shotgun approach, and most of those deals are REO properties. Before I go any further let me explain exactly what an REO property is. REO is an acronym for Real Estate Owned. An REO property is a home that has gone through the foreclosure process, and the bank or entity that held the loan on the home now owns it and they have to sell it in an attempt to recover some or all of the losses they incurred on the bad loan.

The first and biggest problem with REO properties is that banks are not likely to allow you to assign your contract to a new buyer. This means you must first close on the property with your own funds and then turn around and close again with your back end buyer. No problem right? Well maybe. It all depends on your title company and their willingness to work with you, the investor, in transacting LEGAL, above-board, double-closing transactions. Let's assume you have lined up your title company and that you have your private funds arranged to help with funding your short-term deals. This is where correct entity structuring comes into play. You will need to be an owner of record to resell this property. It may turn out that you are only on the chain of title for five minutes, or even a day or so, but *you are still on the chain of title.* This is where your entity tax vehicle can help deflect some of the taxes and put more cash into your pocket (please consult your tax professional and accountant before deciding what entity is best for you).

Another big problem is that offers on REO-owned property must include proof of funds. This may present a problem for newer investors who do not have the appropriate contacts in the hard money world or the credit (see section on *Managing Your Credit* in the Appendix) needed to secure these properties. Once you secure a good private money contact—it can also be private funds from a family member or close friend that you pay interest on—you are one step closer to getting into these REO properties and possibly making some huge gains.

Banks that own these properties often require that a copy of an earnest money check be submitted with every offer you make. This can get expensive real fast if you are making forty to fifty offers per week and you are putting up the minimum earnest money with each. These banks can require $500 to a $1,000 minimum on each offer. This is when you need to be either a real estate licensee or you need to have a good relationship with a licensee who understands your business. This is because in this segment of the business, you need to play the law of large numbers when you are making offers.

You may make 40-50 offers before getting one or two accepted contracts. Most realtors who do not understand what you are doing will get discouraged and not want to work with you because your offers seem too low. They will want you to come up and offer closer to the asking price to get a contract accepted. They do not understand that you—as an investor—are not looking for *marginal* deals; instead, you are looking for one or two *exceptional* deals. So it is best to have a relationship with a realtor who understands this and is willing to make multiple offers knowing that only one or two may get accepted.

If you ask a typical real estate agent to write 40 contracts for you on different properties that you have never even seen, they are going to think you are crazy. To exemplify this, I will tell you a story. I once experimented with an agent who didn't understand what I was doing. We wrote 10 offers, which seemed like a lot to her. She said in a sarcastic tone, "Well, I hope at least one of these gets accepted," and then she laughed. She did not know that I was used to writing 30 offers before getting one accepted. When I finally told her that, she never returned my calls again.

Provide copies of a check with each offer; however, ask them if they are only allowed to cash it if the offer is accepted. The trick here is that you need to furnish the funds once the contract is accepted, or the bank will not take your contract pending, and you will be out of the deal—it could also ruin your relationship with the realtor who is helping you find these great deals. Trust me; finding a realtor who understands the wholesaling business—one who can help you work deals in this lucrative area—can be an extremely valuable tool and very hard to replace.

Strategy in Dealing with Banks

Most major banks use asset companies (that they hire on a nationwide level) to liquidate their REO properties. In the wake of the foreclosure crisis—or *opportunity* as I like to call it—these asset companies, and more importantly these asset managers, are very over-worked. So my strategy in dealing with these REO properties has become a multi-step process. I've outlined that process below, each step with some explanation:

Step 1 – *Don't make an offer on a property unless it has been on the market for at least thirty days.* The reason for this is that as soon as a property is listed on the Multiple Listing Service (MLS), the asset manager can only take off a certain percentage of the list price per his upper management; however, they are usually allowed to make a price reduction after thirty or so days on the MLS. So the trick is to make a low offer on the property right at or just before a price reduction is about to occur. This way you can still get a good price and maybe stay ahead of the competitors who may also be watching the property and waiting to pounce.

Step 2 – *Make your request for a price reduction on the tail end of your inspection period.* This is where it gets kind of tricky, so be careful here. Most asset managers have an IN pile, a PENDING pile, and a CLOSED pile, or something similar. So let's assume you made the offer, timed it right, and now you have a pending deal. If you played your cards right, you got yourself a seven to ten-day (most banks nowadays are only allowing seven days) inspection period. Once your file was marked PENDING, the asset manager moved it over from the IN pile to the PENDING pile. If this is a larger company, that asset manger may have received several more new files in their in pile that they now have to deal with. So when your price reduction of a few thousand dollars reaches them (you are asking for a reduction because your contractor's estimates were higher than you thought—note: I always like to supply actual written estimates and photos of any mold, stolen plumbing or any other nastiness that I can find), there is a good chance they will look at your request and think, *for only a few thousand more, I can get rid of this dog and mark it CLOSED!*

When you do this, you must be willing to remove the inspection contingency and proceed to closing. So if you don't have a buyer lined up for this property at this time, and you placed your earnest money up, then you must be prepared to close on this deal in the allotted time, either with your own funds or by finding a buyer, OR you must be willing to lose your earnest money.

Step 3 – *Make good friends with the REO realtors.* The information in this step could also be included in the How to Find Deals chapter, but I felt it would be better served here, as it is a *strategy* I only use with banks. Any decent REO realtor will have several listings with a few different asset managers. They will have the inside track on listings that are coming up available, and more importantly, listings that are getting ready for a reduction in price. If you make yourself known to them and prove that you are able to close transactions, they will be more than happy to assist you. If you have a license, I'd suggest letting them keep the commissions from the sale since you are more interested in making a much larger fee wholesaling the property anyway. If you help them make more money and close more properties, you will earn their loyalty.

Step 4 – *Prey on the asset managers who are overworked and having a fire sale.* This is where your good REO realtor relationships or just plain luck (if you happen to find one of these on your own) will come into play. When you encounter this situation, you need to move fast and capitalize. What I mean is if you have an asset manager who is approving sales on properties that are spectacular bargains, you need to quickly find out what else that bank has listed in that area. Chances are it is the same asset manager who sold the other property for far below list price. It is likely that a price reduction has not been made on the property, so you need to strike while the opportunity is there. If that bank has another property listed—especially with that same realtor—take a look at it and make an offer that is considerably lower than list price. Chances are you can make yourself a great deal.

Step 5 – *Find the motivated banks.* This is very similar to looking for the overworked asset managers but a little easier to accomplish. I search the multiple listings for banks that are offering selling bonuses to agents (this information is only available to realtors so don't be too shy to ask the realtor you are working with, and after they find out why you want it, they will be happy to help you if it means securing more sales and bonuses for themselves) or repair credits, or any other sales incentive if sold by a certain date. This is important because it indicates that the bank has too much inventory and they need to get some of the money recouped to put back to work in the lending world. Banks are in the money business and those that don't lend money don't make much money. Another key indicator that a bank is motivated is if they are having major financial troubles. This is easy to determine; just turn on any financial news channel and look. I found one of the greatest deals I've ever made when a bank was taken over by the FDIC. This major bank went under for various reasons and it made them extremely motivated to unload their properties; however, the window of opportunity was very short on this. I made it a specific point to search out properties owned by this particular institution and I made my offers. When the window of opportunity closed, I had made three great deals because of this.

Step 6 – *Look for the 4th quarter "Hail Mary" sales.* First, I'll explain how asset companies and banks work. Most banks give their asset companies a limit on the amount of losses they are allowed to absorb in a year. A loss for a bank is simple. Let's assume a bank takes a property back and the loan default amount was $100,000. After the home sits vacant for a year or so before going to sale (time varies from state to state depending on foreclosure laws), it has incurred some damage from theft and lack of maintenance. So the home is now only worth $75,000. After being on the market, it sells for $60,000. The bank has just taken a $40,000 loss. Suppose the REO department is allowed one hundred million in losses for the year. During the first part of the year, the REO department will generally meet their targets and avoid taking too much of a loss on these properties. But when the 4th quarter rolls around (October through December), the REO asset department will see that they may have sixty million in losses they can write off. What is important to realize here is that the bank gives the asset department the familiar policy of "use it or lose it." In other words, what they do not spend that fiscal year will appear as a loss in next year's numbers because the amount will carry over and blow next year's numbers out of the water. Usually the best time to take advantage of this seasonal phenomenon is the start of November and especially in December. This isn't the policy with every bank, but a vast majority of them follow this outline.

The Competition is not Fierce

Because of the rules in the REO-owned properties market, and the requirement of having a slightly higher level of funds available to do deals in this market, much of the competition from other wholesalers is eliminated. These funding requirements make this a tougher realm to work in—you must have either your own funds or private money funds when you make your offers and you may need to have some entities set up for tax and personal protection—but after you get through the red tape and you consistently handle the necessary paperwork, you can be one of the few with a large inventory of excellent properties to chose from.

Beware of Bank Addendums

This section isn't meant to scare the reader away from bank owned properties; rather, is here to raise a certain level of awareness. Once you receive an accepted offer from a bank, the realtor will send you over the bank as-is addendums. These vary by bank, but most have the same content in one form or another. A few key factors will be important to you:

Assignment of Contract – If the bank is a large bank, most likely they will have a clause about not being able to assign your contract. The reason they have this is because they want to know who their buyer is and that the buyer is capable of performing. At least that's the reason they tell you. I believe the real reason is to protect themselves and protect their jobs. If the asset managers are selling the property to you for X dollars and then you assign it to someone else for X + Y dollars, then when the asset manager's boss sees that, they go back to the asset managers and ask why *they* couldn't sell it for the X+Y in the first place and why they only got X. So to protect themselves from this, they say "no assignment of contracts." Sometimes this may be negotiated, especially during the 4th-quarter fire sales, when asset managers have bonuses on the line.

Per Diem charge – This is a nasty gotcha. They like to put this little per diem (which means per day) charge of $100 or so for each day you close outside the contract date. Make sure you are aware of this and what the fee is in case something happens and your deal closes late.

Deed restrictions on the property – This will absolutely kill any wholesaler who is trying to double close. This is one contingency that you cannot possibly have in your contract. Fannie Mae is notorious for this one, so if you are buying a Fannie Mae-owned home, then you must negotiate this item out of the contract. With this deed restriction, the owner cannot sell the property for more than twenty percent of what they purchased the home for in the first ninety days of ownership. They do this to "combat illegal flipping," or so they say. The problem is if you get a great deal and you can make a large profit but this clause is in there, you may be cutting yourself off at the knees. I have successfully negotiated this clause out of contracts for Fannie Mae-owned homes several times. We need to watch for this more now than ever before. As I'm writing this book, Fannie Mae and Freddie Mac were taken over by the federal government. With the potential mortgage bailout going on in our country today, more and more homes will be taken over and sold by Fannie and Freddie, which means this deed restriction will pop up more and more.

Mold disclosure – Even if the home does not have mold, you will get one of these so the bank can have a little CYA on their side.

11 – Wholesaling and Retirement

Most people in the real estate investing world look at wholesaling as a job and not as a way of investing, and in most cases they are correct. In many ways, a wholesaler is just a glorified realtor who is matching up sellers to buyers and turning a profit in the middle. However, I propose a different way of thinking about wholesaling. In other chapters, I discuss various elements of the wholesaling business. Here I am going to discuss them in terms of retirement and long-term investment.

Let's say you successfully wholesale four properties per month and you average $5,000 per deal. After expenses and taxes you may have $14,000 or so per month. But consider this: What if you keep some properties for yourself to build up a retirement? What if you dedicate one entire deal per quarter to this end, and you use the proceeds from that deal to pay down the principal on one of your properties? You will be adding an additional $20,000 per year towards principal on a property. Once you pay that property off, you can work on another one. You can easily see the equity you can amass after a few years, as well as the cash flow you will enjoy by paying it off.

If you love the beauty of leverage, then instead of paying off your properties early, you can use the funds to leverage into additional properties to add to your personal portfolio. This will increase your personal cash flow and your wealth situation. There are many different avenues you can take to use wholesaling as a wealth-building tool. Personally, I use wholesaling in combination. I am always looking for properties either to keep for myself or flip. As I run my normal day-to-day operations, I cherry-pick deals that I want to keep for myself. I like to do buy-and-holds, retails flips, and also investor wholesale flips. Below I'm going to explain each one of these and the benefits of each.

Buy and Hold

This is my favorite strategy, as I'm a firm believer this is one of the greatest wealth-building tools available. This is where you buy a property and hold it for rental purposes. You build wealth from the appreciation and monthly cash flow. Over time, the rents pay down the debt, giving you more equity and appreciation. When you do sell and cash out after sometime, you should have made a return that far exceeds most other forms of long-term investing.

Retail Flips

This is not to be confused with retail shopping centers. Retail flipping is a term used to describe buying a single-family home and fixing it up to sell to a person who is going to live in it. Homebuyers who are shopping for a personal residence are considered retail buyers because they are more concerned with a home's amenities, location and functionality for their families as opposed to functionality of the numbers. Even in this depressed market, retail flips can be successful. I personally do one of these per quarter; however, I cater to first-time homebuyers.

Wholesale Investor Flips

I favor this one over retail flipping. This is a strategy that works best when you have the property pre-sold. When you run an annualized rate of return on this compared to other sell strategies, this one surpasses them all. This is where you buy a property and rehab it to rent-ready standards. You then sell the property to another landlord that needs to secure financing on it. You make less of a mark up than you would on a retail flip, but you move it much faster. You sell it at a price that gives the investor a good deal as well as making you a profit.

If you want to be a successful real estate investor I suggest using all the above strategies to create a nice blended real estate income and portfolio for retirement purposes. No one strategy is better than the other. It all depends on your personal preference.

Appendix

Managing Your Credit

You know that your credit score is extremely important, but do you really know why? Probably not. You should take comfort in the fact that you are not alone. Millions of Americans have no idea how a credit rating, and the credit rating system, really works.

The Importance of Your Credit Score

As a real estate investor in today's challenging market place, why is it so important to fully maximize your credit potential? Whether you are just starting to invest in real estate or you are a 35-year veteran, without a great credit score, you are going to be limited in how many homes you can finance and how well the properties can cash flow. The reason you are purchasing these properties is to either generate passive cash flow from your rentals, or to gain appreciation to add to your portfolio. Great credit is one of the real estate investor's most invaluable tools.

What do we mean by that? Especially now, in this very difficult lending market, lenders have tightened their guidelines and they are extremely cautious about loaning money. One thing that dissolves those fears is a fantastic credit score. With a low credit score, you are much less likely to be approved for a primary residence, much less an investment property.

So how could your credit possibly affect your cash flow on a rental property? Suppose you have an above-average credit rating, and you are approved for the loan, but your banker comes back with a rate of 9.5% because you already own 2 other properties and your credit score is not phenomenal. In this scenario, you will be able to secure the loan but with a high rate of 9.5%, you would have to put a very large amount down on the house in order for your tenant to even be able to cover the mortgage payment, let alone clear it to give you the cash flow you are looking for.

What is considered a phenomenal credit score? The credit scoring range, which was formed by the Fair Isaac Corporation (FICO) is 300-850, 850 being the best. As a real estate investor if your score isn't above at least a 750, you may very well run into the issues listed above.

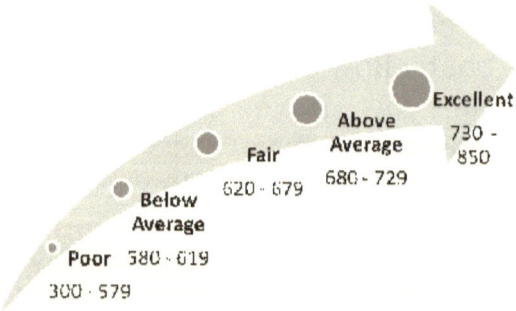

For those of you who already have an 800+ credit score and see no real reason to take on this new information, we have something for you to consider. Do you know why you have an 800 credit score? Do you know how your future ventures will affect your great credit? We can assure you that you didn't get to an 800 credit score by simply paying your bills early. There is a formula that you have been systematically following whether you know it or not.

The Components of Your Credit Score

So now that you know why you need great credit, and you are aware of where your credit really needs to be to thrive in this market, let's look at what your credit score is made up of? There are actually 5 main components. It's probably easiest to think of your credit as a giant pie, and that pie is split up into 5 different sized slices.

#1 - Payment History

The biggest portion accounts for 35% of your credit rating, which is based on your payment history. This is the most important part in determining your credit score. Your payment history simply reflects how you have kept the terms of the loans you have secured.

#2 - Debt-to-Credit Ratio
The second biggest portion, which accounts for 30% of your score, is your debt-to-credit ratio. How much you owe in relation to how much you are able to charge. For example: If you have a credit line of $10,000 and you currently owe $5,000, your credit ratio is 50%. The lower your ratio the better.

#3 - Length of Payment History
15% of your credit rating is based on your length of payment history. This portion is not looking at how you have kept up on the terms of your loans; rather, it reflects the amount of time the account has been open. This is really the only way age plays a part in helping or harming your credit. The longer you have had accounts open the better off you are.

#4 - New Credit or New Accounts
10% of your credit rating is based on new credit or new accounts that have just been opened. An account is no longer considered new credit when it has reached 3 years. This is why it is not wise to open too many accounts at once.

#5 - Types of Credit
The remaining 10% of your credit score is based on the *types* of credit you have. You may think the fact that credit bureaus are interested in diversity is strange, but they want to make sure your report is not dominated by one type of credit. You might ask yourself: "Is my credit history well balanced or do I just have just mortgages or just unsecured debt?"

Lenders are secretive about the structural nature of your credit score because they want to keep you in the dark. The less you know about your credit and how to improve your score, the more money they make on high interest rates. Every citizen deserves to understand how the credit industry really works inside and out.

You may or may not have bad credit, but either way, one thing is for sure: you realize just how imperative your credit score is to buying the things you want and living the life you want. Those three little numbers dictate your chances of buying a house, buying a car, getting a credit card, and maybe even getting a job. You want to have a better credit score. Am I right? Whether you think your credit is so bad that you don't even bother to check your score, or you are just looking to bring your score up an extra notch, you can do so with the help of a credit coach.

Once you thoroughly understand how the credit bureaus rate your credit, you will not only be able to correct discrepancies in your credit records, you can also avoid the credit mistakes that led to those discrepancies in the first place. The credit industry has always seemed vague, almost mysterious. How do they calculate credit scores, are all credit reports the same, should you be opening up more credit or closing out unused cards? Although credit scoring does not always seem like it follows the rules of common sense, it is not rocket science either. Anyone can learn how to play the credit score game.

Using a Credit Professional

Taryn Donnelly is the president and founder of *Your Credit Consulting Expert*, a national company with an excellent program dedicated to educating people on how to make the best possible choices to improve their credit. The focus of her program is to make credit improvement easy to understand with accurate, useful, and practical information, so that anyone can make knowledgeable decisions about their financial future.

Taryn's background in the mortgage industry and her strong understanding of credit, makes her an expert in her field. She has helped hundreds of families secure their dream homes with the information she has been perfecting for 7 years. Taryn has studied America's credit industry from the inside, and she can give you the TRUTH about your credit.

Taryn and her team will teach you proven methods that have worked for countless others. Her coaching programs are packed with everything from *what makes up your credit scores* to *maintaining your perfect credit.* After working with her, you will be able to answer the toughest credit questions for yourself. Upon completion of her program, you will have all the information you need to maintain perfect credit for the rest of your life.

There are many misconceptions about how credit reporting really works. Taryn and her team address the misinformation. They educate you on exactly what makes up your credit score, how you can avoid the costly mistakes that most real estate investors make, and how you can improve your credit score for life. Once you realize that your credit score is determined by your financial behavior, you realize that you hold the key to your own credit success.

For more information, about Taryn's products and services you can log on to www.yourcreditconsultingexpert.com. For more valuable credit tips you can sign up for free monthly newsletters.

Additional Notes on Business Structure

(Information in this section provided by Oak Hill Financial Group, Inc.)

Many entrepreneurs have two goals when choosing a structure for their business: 1) protecting their personal assets from business claims (limited liability) and 2) having business profits taxed on their individual tax returns. S corporations limit owners' liability and offer the tax structure of a partnership.

S Corporations

Not long ago, an S corporation was the only choice for these business owners. In recent years, however, limited liability companies (LLCs) have for the most part replaced S corporations. Still, some businesses can benefit by organizing as S corporation.

What Is an S Corporation?

An S corporation is a regular corporation that has elected "S corporation" tax status. Forming an S corporation lets you enjoy the limited liability of a corporate shareholder but pay income taxes as if you were a sole proprietor or a partner. In a regular corporation (also known as a "C corporation"), the company itself is taxed on business profits. The owners also pay individual income tax on money they receive from the corporation as salary, bonuses, or dividends. So revenues sort of get taxed twice: once at the corporate level and again at the individual level.

By contrast, in an S corporation, all business profits "pass through" to the owners, who report them on their personal tax returns (as in sole proprietorships, partnerships, and LLCs). The S corporation itself does not pay any income tax, although an S corporation with more than one owner must file an informational tax return—like a partnership or LLC—to report each shareholder's portion of the corporate income.

Most states follow the federal pattern when taxing S corporations: They don't impose a corporate tax, choosing instead to tax the business's profits on the shareholders' personal tax returns. About half a dozen states, however, tax an S corporation like a regular corporation. The tax division of your state treasury department can tell you how S corporations are taxed in your state.

Should You Elect S Corporation Status?
Operating as an S corporation may be wise for several reasons:
Forming an S corporation generally allows you to pass business losses through to your personal income tax return, where you can use them to offset any income that you (and your spouse, if you are married) have from other sources.

Also, when you sell your S corporation, your taxable gain on the sale of the business can be less than it would have been had you operated the business as a regular corporation. And S corporation shareholders are not subject to self-employment taxes (active LLC owners are). These taxes, which add up to more than 15% of your income, are used to pay your Social Security and Medicare taxes.

Aside from the benefits, S corporations impose strict requirements. Here are the main rules:

- Each S corporation shareholder must be a U.S. citizen or resident.
- S corporations may not have more than 100 shareholders.
- S corporation profits and losses may be allocated only in proportion to each shareholder's interest in the business.
- An S corporation shareholder may not deduct corporate losses that exceed his or her "basis" in

corporate stock—which equals the amount of the shareholder's investment in the company plus or minus a few adjustments.

- S corporations may not deduct the cost of fringe benefits provided to employee-shareholders who own more than 2% of the corporation.

Fortunately, a decision to elect to be an S corporation isn't permanent. If your business later becomes more profitable and you find there are tax advantages to being a regular corporation, you can drop your S corporation status after a certain amount of time.

Limited Liability Companies (LLCs)
The advantages of forming an LLC are that the members are afforded limited liability and have pass-through taxes similar to a partnership.

By forming an LLC instead of a corporation, you get all the benefits of forming a corporation, but you avoid a few drawbacks you would run into if you formed a corporation. Specifically, when you form a corporation, you subject yourself to double taxation and excessive paperwork. Both of those annoyances can be avoided if you form an LLC.

How do LLCs work?
The LLC allows for multiple owners, or members. Additionally, there is a managing member, who also enjoys the rewards of limited liability and is typically the person responsible for managing the business. However, if the LLC has just one owner, it will be taxed as a sole proprietorship.

The profits or losses of the business pass directly through to the owners' personal income tax returns, on their Form 1040. The LLC files a Form 1065 and then lists each member's taxable profit on Form K-1. In other words, the LLC itself does not file taxes.

This is what we mean when we say you avoid double taxation with an LLC. In a corporation, it works differently. The corporation is taxed and, accordingly, must file taxes. Then, distributions to the owners are taxed. In essence, the government takes two bites out of your revenues instead of the one bite they'll take if you form an LLC instead of a corporation.

With an LLC, the bottom-line profit of the business is not considered earned income to the members, and therefore it is not subject to self-employment tax. But keep in mind that the managing member's share of the bottom-line profit of the LLC is considered earned income, and therefore it is subject to self-employment tax.

Members are compensated using either distributions of profit or guaranteed payments. A distribution of profit allows each member to pay themselves by merely writing checks—whenever they need the money (provided the business has the available cash). However, as a member of an LLC, you are not allowed to pay yourself wages.

Guaranteed payments represent earned income to the members, thereby qualifying them to enjoy the benefits of tax-favored fringe benefits. The members' share of bottom-line profit is not considered earned income because the members are considered to be inactive owners; therefore, the members do not qualify for special tax-favored "fringe benefit" treatment.

A corporation can be a member of an LLC. This allows you to create an additional level of ownership, which is designed to create an entity that can offer such traditional fringe benefits as retirement plans and an additional level of protection from liability.

The managing member of an LLC can deduct 100 percent of the health insurance premiums he or she pays—up to the extent of their pro-rata share of the LLC's net profit, because the profit is considered earned income. Note: If a member has earned income, he or she will also qualify.

So are there any disadvantages to an LLC? Why isn't every corporation in the world switching to LLC status? Why are traditional C corporations and S corporations still being formed? There are a few answers to that question.

The bottom line is that LLCs are an excellent form of organization that is growing in popularity. If the state you operate in allows the creation of LLCs and you can use the features it offers, yet you don't want all of the paperwork and costs associated with incorporating, it's worth learning about LLC benefits and LLC drawbacks.

About Oak Hill Financial Group, Inc.
Jay H. Millard, MBA is principal of Oak Hill Financial Group, Inc., an independent tax accounting and financial planning firm located in Bellevue, KY. He can be reached at (859) 291-0222. Jay is dedicated to providing

competent, objective tax, business and financial advice to people from all walks of life, on an hourly as-needed basis. There are no account minimums or long-term contracts required. Jay focuses on working with two often overlooked and underserved markets: (1) middle-income individuals and families, and (2) do-it-yourselfers who need or want occasional professional advice or a second opinion. Many people who have previously been turned away by traditional asset management or financial planning firms with high minimums will be pleased to know that, through Jay Millard and Oak Hill Financial Group, Inc., they now have access to the same quality financial planning and advice once available only to the wealthy.

Calculating Maximum Allowable Offer

I'm going to show you how I calculate my Maximum Allowable Offer (MAO) for wholesale deals and flip deals.

Calculating MAO'S on Wholesale Deals
If you're doing a wholesale deal, you need to figure out two variables: 1) what percentage of the ARV you're going to offer your deals at, and 2) how much money you want to charge for your wholesale deal

As far as percentage, I like to use the 65% ARV to my investor, meaning a percentage of whatever the home is worth in fixed up condition. Lets say it will be $100,000. That means the investor will have no more than $65,000 total invested in the property. Now let's assume that the property needs $20,000 worth of repairs and I am going to sell the property for $45,000. So $45,000.00

+ $20,000 equals the $65,000 total invested.

As far as the second variable in calculating the MAO, how much money you want to charge for your wholesale deal, let's assume you want to make a $10,000 wholesale fee on a deal. In practice, this number will change from deal to deal, but we will use it for this example. I normally use $100,000 to make math easy; however, I am going to use a realistic value to show you how it works in a live deal scenario.

MAO calculation - wholesale property:

Property Value:	$78,000
Investor's all-in cost (purchase + renovations)*:	$50,700
Needed Renovations	$15,000
Price investor can pay for property	$35,700

* This is 65% of the 78,000.00 ARV

You calculate this last value by taking the investor's all-in cost and subtracting the renovations. This is what you can charge the investor for the property based on the needed renovations while keeping them at the target 65% of the after-repair value invested.

Maximum Allowable Offer: $25,700

This is where you take the money you want to make on the assignment fee (your profit); in this example we used $10,000 and subtract it from what your investor will pay as a purchase price, which we calculated to be $35,700. If you were trying to target $5,000, profit then your MAO would be adjusted to $30,700.

So now we have our MAO for a piece of property; however, this doesn't mean you automatically offer that full amount. I generally start offering 30% below my MAO on a property. So for this example, my first initial offer to the seller would be $17,990. Remember: do not take into account what the property is listed for. We don't care what the list price is; our only concern is how much we are willing to pay in order for the deal to work for us. If the seller does not accept our offer because it is too low, then move on to the next property. This is where making several offers on several properties helps because we are playing the law of large numbers looking for a couple of good deals that will work with our numbers.

I know you are thinking: *If you make offers on properties that you don't even see how can you begin to calculate the MAO?* This is where I kind of work in reverse. Once I make several offers based on the preset formula I use, which is just under half of the list price, and get a contract accepted, I calculate the ARV by running comps and determine the amount of money an investor will have into the property to reach that 65% of the ARV mark.

I then go into the home and calculate the repairs needed to make the home appraise for the maximum ARV. I then subtract the amount of money I want to make, or my wholesale fee. Once I have these figures, I determine if the offer I have accepted is good or if I need to request a price reduction from the seller to reach my targeted goal.

So one of my wholesale formulas will look something like this, based on the above example with just one more step.

Accepted contract price:	$28,000
Property Value:	$78,000
Investor's all in price:	$50,700
Needed Renovations:	$15,000
Sale price to Investor:	$35,700
Wholesale fee (my profit):	$10,000
MAO (or maximum purchase price):	$25,700
Price reduction from seller for deal to work:	$2,300

Calculate this by taking the already accepted contract price of $28,000 and subtracting my maximum allowable offer. Again, this additional step is only needed when you make offers in volume before viewing the homes first. If your dealing with banks, and you follow the instructions in the wholesaling and REO properties chapter, this price reduction should be easy to accomplish.

Calculating MAO'S on Flip Deals

These are calculated in almost the same fashion as the above deal; however, there are a couple other costs (or variables) to determine. In this case, you will need to determine at what price you are going to sell the home for. Being a retail flip I try for a higher percentage of the ARV than I use with a wholesale deal. I market my retail flips at 80% of the ARV, and I'm willing to sell for 75% of the ARV.

You also need to determine the rate of return you're trying to make on your money, or the flat rate amount of cash you're trying to reach. My rule is no less than 20% profit margin. Then you have to factor in repairs. On a retail flip deal, you have several more costs to factor in, the big one being holding costs. While you renovate and market the property for sale, you have holding costs. These costs are: 1) interest on your loan, 2) taxes, 3) insurance and 4) utility costs. Another expense is the costs to market and sell it. These include any advertising you may do, and real estate commissions if you sell it through a realtor in some fashion.

MAO calculation - retail flip property:

Market value of the home	$120,000
Listing price of home (80% of market value)	$96,000
Likely sale price of home (75% of market value)	$90,000
Marketing fee's (6% realtor commission)	$5,400
Holding cost (calculating 4-month hold time) Includes interest on private money, pro-ration of taxes, and utilities	$4,000
Net proceeds after marketing and holding	$80,600
Renovations	$20,000
Net proceeds after all costs	$60,400
Cost associated excluding purchase	$29,400
MAO assuming 20% profit	$38,000

I then add my MAO + renovation cost, and come up with $67,400. I subtract that figure from the net proceeds after marketing and holding costs, and I get the figure of $13,200. Divide that number by the $67,400 to arrive at a 19.8% profit margin, or just under 20%. Do the calculations with different numbers to see if you can reach your desired rate of return. You can run the numbers up until that point and plug in different purchase prices until the numbers come out to where you want them. Your MAO represents the most you can pay for that particular property. You then start lower than that and work your way up.

Remember, it does not matter what a property is listed for. The only thing we're concerned with is how much we are willing to pay.

Common Terms

As is where is – A term used by sellers, primarily banks, that indicates you are buying a property "as is," with no warranties and no promises by the sellers to make any repairs. It is sort of like a "word of caution" in the real estate business.

Auto prospect – the multiple listing service has an "auto prospecting" feature that will email you listings depending on the criteria your agent enters for you. If you arer looking for 3-5 bedrooms in xyz area, then auto prospecting will automatically email new listings as they come up.

Assignment – Mostly used in the world of real estate wholesaling. It refers to the act of assigning a contract to purchase of a piece of property from one party to another

ARV – After Repair Value – what a property is worth after it is fixed up.

Back side of a deal – refers to a wholesale deal in which there is a double closing. This is the second part of 2 transactions and refers to the re-sell of the property to your investor.

Bank as-is addendums – Banks paperwork you fill out when you buy one of their homes. They sell all property as is where is with no warranties. They will make you sign acknowledgements to this.

Bird Dog – a person who looks for deals and brings them to you, and for that service, you pay them a fee if the deal is successful and closes.

Bridge loan – A bridge loan often refers to a commercial property or investment property that may be in transition and does not yet qualify for traditional financing. A bridge loan resembles a hard-money loan because they both have similar criteria for approval and similar costs to the borrower.

Broker – Uses as a noun, "broker" can refer to a couple different people: 1) a person who has a real estate brokerage (often meaning they own it), and 2) a person who is a mortgage broker and brokers loans on properties. A broker is a real estate agent that has a license to open their own business and have other agents work for them.

Broker (Used as a verb, as in, "to broker a deal") – when a real estate agent represents a buyer or seller in a transaction.

Buy and hold strategy – to buy a property and keep it for rental purposes to generate cash flow and equity.

Cap rate – Percentage of return that the property performs at.

Carrying costs – Expenses you have while you own a property. Examples could include taxes, insurance, utilities, and any interest on a mortgage.

Cash flow rental property – a rental property that—after all the expenses are paid—still produces money left over in profit. This left over money is your cash flow.

Cash on cash return – the amount of annualized return you earn on your hard money that you put into a deal.

Chain of title – The record of ownership of a piece of property kept in court records.

Cash-positioned – a person or entity that has cash on hand to readily invest. This may be someone who just sold some property or liquidated some other asset and has cash to invest.

Commercial property – Several types of property fall into this category. First, it can be any property with five or more living units. For example, apartment buildings are considered commercial property. Commercial properties can also be:

- Retail centers
- Office Buildings
- Medical buildings
- Hotels
- Any type of property that will house a business or a warehouse of some sort

Comp – A *comp*arable sale of a similar property. Comps are used to determine a subject property's value. For example, on a house appraisal, several "comps" would be used as references in determining the value of the property being appraised.

Construction draws – Your lender may give you money for work done to the property as part of the loan agreement. These are construction draws.

Contract pending – Bank will not take your contract if it is pending to many contingencies.

Conventional loan – Conventional loans are primarily made for residential or commercial property.

Cost book - Books written to give an idea of what general contracting costs and material costs are across the county. Good for any novice person getting handyman services or repairs so that they do not over-pay.

Database – A list of your clients, including all of their contact information. Databases can refer to several things: 1) a list of available properties, 2) clients, or other types of information. It is a centralized list of information you gather about a subject or people.

Debt Service – monthly payment on a house you pay to lender.

DOM – Days On Market – amount of days a property has been on sale.

Double closing – the act of purchasing a property and then reselling it moments later. Both sales are recorded on the chain of title.

Dry closing – The act of doing a closing where no funds are brought to the table or disbursed at that time but are set for a later time to fund.

Equity gained – when you get a property with 40k or so equity in it and you keep it in your portfolio. That is $40,000 in "equity gained."

Equity position – this refers to a real estate person or seller getting a piece of ownership in a deal structured in for them. For example if a commercial realtor sells a 10 million dollar property and the commission is 2 percent, they may opt instead for 1 percent commission and a piece of ownership of the property. This is called getting an equity position.

First lien position – On a deed, the primary lender will be recorded *first*, giving them first lien position. If there is a foreclosure, then the first lien position must be satisfied before the second lien position is satisfied. Therefore, the first position is the most secure position on the title.

Flip – to buy a property, renovate it, and then resell it for a profit.

Foreclosure – the process in which a bank takes back a piece of property because of the mortgagor's failure to pay.

Front side of a deal – refers to a wholesale deal in which there is a double closing. If you must first close as the buyer with a bank or seller then that is known as the "front side of the deal" since that part is taking place up front, before you can re-sell the property.

General contracted Out – Hiring a general contractor to perform your renovation work.

Hard money – actual cash from a bank account ready to lend from a private lender. You can be a hard-money lender if you have cash that you can lend to someone to purchase property.

Hard-Money loan – A hard-money loan is a specific type of asset-based, loan financing in which a borrower receives funds secured by the value of a parcel of real estate. Hard-money loans are typically issued at much higher interest rates than conventional commercial or residential property loans and are almost never issued by a commercial bank or other deposit institution. Hard money loans are similar to a bridge loan. Both loan types share the same criteria for loan approval, and the cost to the borrower is about the same. The primary difference is that a bridge loan often refers to a commercial property or investment property that may be in transition and does not yet qualify for traditional financing, whereas a hard-money loan often refers to not only an asset-based loan with a high interest rate, but possibly a distressed financial situation such as a property for which the owner is in arrears on the existing mortgage, or for which bankruptcy and foreclosure proceedings are occurring. Many hard-money mortgages are made by private investors, generally in their local areas. Depending on the particular lender, the credit score of the borrower may or may not be important, as the loan is secured by the value of the collateral property. Typically, the maximum loan-to-value ratio on a hard-money loan is 65-70%.

Hard-money world – this is a subculture of hard-money lenders and people who are associated with it. They have their own lending terms and criteria.

Income producing property – Not to be confused with investment property because not all investment properties produce income. An income producing property is any property that produces income from tenants who occupy or use the space, be it residents or a business that may pay some type of rent.

Investment property – This can be any property purchased for investment purposes (usually refers to a property that will be held for a longer period of time and not flipped). From single family, to an office building, to a 200-unit apartment complex, to a retail strip center.

Law of large numbers – This is used in various types of business and refers to doing something enough times that you will produce the desired results over the long run. For example, telemarketers use this concept daily when they make a large amount of calls trying to sell their product. If they call a large number of prospects, they will make a significant number of sales. If they have a 1% success ratio then they are working the law of large numbers. Ask as many as possible and achieve a certain percentage.

Licensee – A person who holds a professional license. In the world of wholesaling, a licensee usually refers to a person with a real estate license.

Local board contract – standardized real estate contracts that are used by realtors from different companies that are members of that particular board.

LOI – Letter Of Intent – A simply drafted letter stating terms and conditions to purchase a piece of property. Commonly used in commercial real estate. This is important to know in case you get into wholesaling apartment communities or other types of commercial property.

Loan-to-Value (LTV) Ratio – For example, if a property is worth $100,000, the lender would advance $65,000-$70,000 against it. This low LTV provides added security for the lender, in case the borrower does not pay and they have to foreclose on the property.

MAO – Maximum Allowable Offer. This is the most you can offer on a property and still make the wholesale fee/profit that you're trying to obtain.

Maintenance – fixing things such as leaky toilets, faucets etc. Good yearly figure to use is 10% of the Estimated Market Rental Value.

MLS – Multiple Listing Service. A tool used by realtors to access listings from other companies in one centralized database. To access the MLS, you must become a member and pay dues or membership fees. Many MLS systems exist across the United States and a particular agent may have access to one or multiple MLS systems. The MLS database can also used for running comparable sales (also known as comps) and gathering other data on a property.

Move-up buyer – a buyer that is moving up from a starter-type home to a nicer, possibly larger, home—usually to accommodate a growing family of sorts. Possibly the buyer makes more money now and wants a nicer home etc.

MLS shotgun approach – This is the act of looking in the MLS and finding several properties to make offers on. These are properties that you haven't even seen or been inside. You are just making a large amount of offers looking for a few motivated sellers.

MLS Comp – See *Comp*

Net operating income – amount of cash left over after you pay expenses. Also referred to as cash flow.

Open Line – This is an open line of credit. Kind of like an equity line of credit from a bank. It's open and you draw from it and pay it down and then you can draw more.

Out-of-pocket cash – this is how much hard cash you put into a deal. Example: if you are buying a $100,000 house and they want a 10% down payment, then your out-of-pocket cash is %10,000.

Pack – A property pack is the paperwork you put together when advertising a property for sale. A pack will include information such as value of the property, price of the property, needed repairs, and rental information.

Point – one point is one percent on a loan. So a point on 100,000 dollars refers to 1,000 dollars.

Pre-selling – building up a buyers reservation list and having a piece of property for them ready to buy before you have even bought it and rehabbed it.

Private money – money that is given to a business or investor from a private individual. This is an investment in the business and is usually not secured by a real estate property. Many private money loans originate from persons with money in some sort of self-directed IRA.

Promissory note – a note that makes a promise to pay back loaned money within an allotted amount of time and at a specified interest rate.

Proof of funds – a letter or copy of a bank statement that shows you have a certain amount of money for funds available.

Rate of return – the percentage your money earns in a one-year period. For example, if you invest 20k and make a 2k profit, then your rate of return is 10%.

Referral – referring someone to another professional for services.

Referral funds – Monies collected from a referral. For example I refer you to another realtor in a different market and they pay me a fee for the business referral.

Rehab – Used as a verb, this refers to the process of making the repairs that a property needs. Used as a noun, it refers to the repairs that a property is undergoing.

Rent factor – The percentage of monthly rental income compared to the total amount of money invested in a property. For example, if an investor has a total of $100,000 invested in a property (note: this includes any purchase + renovations), a rent of $1,500 per month would give it a rent factor of .015.

REO – **Real Estate Owned** – **REO Property** – property a bank owns.

REO realtor – a real estate licensee who works as a listing agent of foreclosed homes for various banks and asset companies. Most REO realtors do not work for exclusively for banks; however, the bank is one of their clients. Some REO agents may work as listing agents for several different banks.

Repair credit – sellers will give funds back to make repairs.

Residential property – This refers to a single-family house that has been designed for residential occupation. In the world of real estate, investing, and with loan originations, any property that is 4 units or less is considered residential. In other words, a two-family home (also known as duplex), a three-family home (also knows as triplex), or a four-family home (also known as quad) are all considered residential properties.

Retail flip – to buy a property, renovate it, and sell it to an end user, also known as a homeowner or owner-occupied

SP – Sale price

Subject to deal (Subject to Existing Financing) – the act of buying a home subject to leaving the existing financing in place. Similar to an *assumption of*

mortgage, but not putting the mortgage in your name.

Sub-market – this is a particular neighborhood in a city. For example the market I invest in is Cincinnati Ohio, but a sub-market in my area is a neighborhood called North College Hill.

Selling bonus – a selling bonus for agents. Banks give these bonuses as an incentive to get it sold.

Short sale – the process in which a financial intuition is taking less than what is owed on the property to avoid a foreclosure

Tax (with respect to pricing a deal) – property taxes

Title company – This is a type of company that will run title searches on a property and do the actual paperwork for closings. Depending on the state you are located in this may be a company that hires out an attorney (known as title states) or an actual lawyer that runs the title company.

Title search – title company act of "clearing out a title," or searching to ensure the property is marketable, and there are no parties who already own an interest in it or have a lien against it.

Trip fees – charges or fees you pay for someone making a trip to the property to check on work progress.

Vacancy – when your home is not rented. Generally a good vacancy rate to use for a year is 10%.

Vanilla, owner-occupied deal – traditional, real estate purchase in which the buyer is purchasing the home to live in. They have excellent credit and are putting down the traditional 20% down payment

Wet closing – Opposite of a dry closing. Funds are brought in for both sides of the transaction.

Wholesale – selling ones interest in a property to another, where both parties are profiting from the equity.

Wholesale fee – amount of money a property wholesaler makes on a deal.

Wholesale investor flip – to buy property, renovate it, and sell it to another landlord who is using a buy and hold strategy. The wholesale investor flip generally does not have as much margin as what exists in a retail flip, but the time between buy and sell is usually less.